"This could be the answer to most of the complaints we hear everyday in this country"

Absolutely Brilliant.

"This is the book the country has been impatiently awaiting."

Why has it taken so long for somebody to figure this out?

"The country has some severe problems, from violent crime to the deficit. I can not think of one major problem that this book does not solve!"

I believed that the ideas in this book were much to controversial to be contemplated .... until I read it.

The Drug Solution just might work.

This book really MUST be read to be appreciated. Mark Greer has an answer to our problems. At the very least this concept should be debated by our society.

I can't believe that this book changed my mind about how we should address our drug problem.

Read this book then send a copy to your Congressman!

THE

DRUG
SOLUTION

How we can Use the Profits from Illicit
Drug sales to *SOLVE* every Major Problem Faced by our Society Today!

WITHOUT RAISING TAXES

By Mark Greer

R.F.T.I.PUBLISHING,
PORTERVILLE CALIFORNIA

THE

DRUG SOLUTION

How we can Use the Profits from Illicit Drug sales to _SOLVE_ every Major Problem Faced by our Society Today!

WITHOUT RAISING TAXES

Published by:

R.F.T.I.
PUBLISHING
P. O. Box 651
Porterville CA 93257 U.S.A.

Copyright © 1994 by Mark Greer
First Printing 1994
Printed in the United States of America

Library of Congress Information

Greer, Mark L.
The Drug Solution -
Mark Greer - First Edition
Bibliography: p3
1. Social Problems / Solutions
2. Current Events
3. Politics
4. Drug Use / Abuse
**Library of Congress Card Catalog Number
LCCC 94-65041
ISBN 0-9640123-7-5 $19.95 Softcover
ISBN 0-9640123-8-3 $27.95 Hardcover**

ACKNOWLEDGEMENTS

This book could not have been completed without the support and help of many of my friends and family members.

The risk you take in acknowledging some is that you may forget others. With that risk in mind, I will still attempt to cover all bases.

Robin Cramer took on the mighty task of editing my manuscript with little more than a promise of good things to come when it became a success.

Sincere thanks to my loving and supportive family, **Sue, Tal, Dineen, Diana, and Janice.** Their support and encouragement was the catalyst that made this book possible. All of the **Panattonis** and **Kincaids** are hereby thanked as well.

Bob Holmes was "the money man." He was instrumental in arranging financing when few would listen to my promises of unbridled success.

Thanks also to my talented cover artist **Laura Kamieniecki** o f **Creative Waves** and my account executive **Jerry Bayley** o f **Delta Lithograph**

To all of the above I owe my current success and happiness.

My sincere and heartfelt thanks to one and all.

Table of Contents

PREFACE

Aren't you getting just a little tired of it all?

Aren't you tired of hearing politicians saying, "Just one more tax increase and everything will be OK?"

Aren't you tired of watching the evening news, and hearing about yet another recently released criminal perpetrating yet another heinous act on some poor innocent?

Aren't you tired of hearing about drugs, and drug use, and listening to our politicians pontificate about what needs to be done? And then realizing that **nothing ever seems to get done?**

Tired of worrying about your family, their safety, and what this country is coming to?

The United States is currently in the throws of a recession. Our crime rate has increased drastically. Drug usage and gang violence are rampant, public safety is a thing of the past. And we have a deficit and debt that is bankrupting our country.

WHY??

We are the wealthiest nation in the world. We have a lifestyle, people, and even climate that is the envy of the world. Our productivity is outstanding, our politicians certainly have enough of our money to spend. So what's the problem?

The objective of this book is to lay out a workable cure for our current fiscal crisis while, at the same time, providing a solution to many of our social ills.

This book shows that **there is a way,** if properly implemented, to completely revitalize our country, our infrastructure, and our inner cities, to quickly eliminate our federal deficit, to provide needed social services, drug rehabilitation facilities, create the finest health care system in the world, to eliminate organized crime and gang activity, solve our prison crisis, make our streets safe again, and even to have a police force that is actually respected and enforces the law.

ALL WITHOUT RAISING TAXES!

Within these pages, a case is made for taxing the profits on illegal drug sales and redirecting those profits to the betterment of the country.

While these ideas are controversial, the facts speak for themselves. We need a complete revision of our drug laws. Using the profits generated from drug sales to solve most of our other social ills is an idea whose time has come.

This is not a book on drug legalization. It is much more. It is an analysis of the costs associated with the drug war and the incredible social benefits that could be realized by passing one well-written law that accomplishes a complete reversal of our current ineffective policies.

This book has been written for those of us who feel frustrated by the impotence of our current efforts to solve the problems of our times. **This is a tall order, but it CAN be accomplished.** Within these pages are the ideas for solving virtually every major social problem we currently face.

The book is structured in a logical format. It begins by offering an in depth description of how we got to where we are with our current drug policies. Following we discuss types and effects of most of the drugs used in this country. We then study our current methods of trying to control drug use and sales in the United States, followed by a discussion of why these methods **don't and can't** work.

Next we go into the heart of the philosophy of **THE DRUG SOLUTION.** How can we use this problem, in a positive way, to solve all our other difficulties? We also provide a detailed description of how the program would work.

Finally, we cover the methods we must implement in order to turn the program into reality. We also offer a chapter on dealing with drug problems as well as resources for solving drug related problems.

The importance of this book cannot be overestimated. It is nothing less than a chance for our country to return to the days, not so long ago, when we could leave our houses unlocked, let our kids play in the park, and had a police force that was both respected and appreciated. The dream of a return to a country with a solid family unit, no deficit, and a secure future, could easily be realized, **IF WE TAKE AC-TION.**

READ THIS INTRODUCTION

This book is written to encourage changes in our drug laws which could revolutionize our entire country. It may well be the most important book you read this year, possibly the most important book you will ever read.

A serious attempt has been made to distance the ideas in this edition from books on simple "Drug Legalization". This book presents a number of unique ideas that can solve **EVERY** major problem we face in this country today.

It is worth noting that the author has no hidden agenda. He is not a frustrated drug user trying to get his particular drug of choice legalized. He neither uses nor advocates the use of any psycho-active substance. He is, in fact opposed to the use of alcohol, nicotine, marijuana, barbiturates, amphetamines, and all mind altering substances, legal and illegal. He does admit to a weakness for a good cup of coffee and will occasionally indulge in a quality cigar.

One effective method of determining the viability of **THE DRUG SOLUTION** is to ask ourselves three questions. First, are we in favor of drug legalization? For most citizens the immediate and emphatic answer is NO. Second, are we in favor of drug legalization if it directly benefits us as individuals and our country in general? The answer to this question may be "probably not" or "tell me more". Third, would we be in favor of a program that allowed those who wish to purchase drugs to do so, if the result would be to eliminate or

15

drastically reduce gang activity, violent crime, the deficit, organized crime, prison and court overcrowding, and unemployment as major concerns in this nation? The answer to this question must be yes or, if not, it likely will be by the time you finish this book.

Another very important question is how do we accomplish these crucial objectives? The ideas proposed in this book will answer this question and much more. Implementing the ideas proposed herein could easily eliminate the deficit, gangs, unemployment, organized crime and practically every other negative aspect of our great country.

What we have to gain includes safe streets, a reduced tax burden, respect for law enforcement, the return of hope to our inner cities, and financial stability, to name but a few of the potential rewards of **THE DRUG SOLUTION.**

Implementation of **THE DRUG SOLUTION** will also provide the funding of programs which support the family. Crime prevention, after all, begins in the home.

A background knowledge of drugs, and drug use is a prerequisite for taking a logical look at how we can address this problem. It is, therefore necessary to gain this knowledge by studying the opening chapters. Even though the real rewards of this book are found in the later chapters, the constant referral back to the basic information found in earlier chapters make chapters One through Four indispensable.

The book opens with a history of drug use in America and proceeds through an overview of the various types of drugs currently in use in America and their various effects on those who choose to use them.

We then review our current methods of distribution, attempts at enforcement, and treatment methods, and briefly discuss why we can NEVER totally eliminate drug use in a free society.

Next, we encapsulate and define what our actual problem is, and examine the hypocrisy of our current laws. We ask how a society that condones alcohol and tobacco can justify the laws against other, less harmful, substances. Next we suggest a workable solution to our current dilemma, and elaborate on how best to implement that solution in a simple and realistic manner.

We suggest that you read through the entire book even if you are familiar with some of the subject matter. The opening chapters provide the groundwork, basis, and statistics on which the fascinating theory of **THE DRUG SOLUTION** is based.

Chapter

One

A HISTORY OF DRUG USE IN AMERICA

Mind-altering substances have been with us since early man and it is very unlikely that their popularity will decrease or cease in the near future. In early American history, the hallucinogen peyote was used in the tribal rituals of many North American Indian tribes. Opium and morphine were the drugs of choice for many maladies such as pain, insomnia, anxiety, malaria,and even tuberculosis, from as early as 1750.

One of the first indications of the serious problems associated with drug addiction became evident during the Civil War. Morphine was used indiscriminantly to relieve the symptoms of everything from syphilis to amputation. The end result was an estimated 200,000 to 400,000 addicts, at the turn of the century.

In 1906 Congress passed the Pure Food and Drug Act requiring that ingredients be listed on the labels of ingested substances. The first actual attempt to control narcotics came in 1909 and 1912 at what was called The Hague Convention in Hague, Netherlands. At this meeting, 34 nations agreed to limit the import of narcotics and allow their use solely for medical purposes. **This was the first rudimentary step in what was to become a 75 year war against the use of narcotics in the United States.**

Delegates from this convention convinced congress to pass a law restricting the use of both opium and cocaine. The U.S. law to control these substances was known as the Harrison act and became effective in February of 1915. This law had little effect on reducing the use of drugs due to the fact that it allowed uncontrolled access to physicians and dentists, many of which continued to prescribe the drugs to addicts. Pharmacists were also allowed to prescribe the drugs and did so virtually upon request. The motivations toward the prescribing of these drugs ranged from genuine concern for patients to outright greed and corruption.

The inability of addicts to obtain drugs was the precursor of our current multi-billion dollar black market in illegal drugs. This situation was compounded by the Supreme Court decision in 1919 of **WEBB vs UNITED STATES** in which the dispensing of drugs to addicts, simply because they were addicts, was outlawed. Numerous laws, both state and federal were subsequently passed in an attempt to control the use of the many and varied narcotic substances on the market.

The 1960's brought on the advent of the "Hippie Generation", as well as numerous other counter cultures and subcultures. The popularity of drug use among these groups was a major factor in leading to the current attitudes toward recreational drug use.

Prior to 1960's, recreational drug use was confined to a minority of the population. The 1960's, however, was a watershed decade. The use of most illegal drugs increased tolerance for a wide range of unconventional behavior. This included the growth of movements that stood in opposition to the war in Vietnam and to mainstream American culture. The coming into popularity of rock music and its attendant lifestyle, and enormous media publicity devoted to drugs, drug users, and drug dealers caused a vigorous drug subculture to come into existence.

During this time some social groups viewed drug use in positive terms. Individuals were evaluated on the basis of whether or not they used illegal drugs, and believed it a virtue to "turn on" someone who did not use drugs. This subculture was a powerful force in recruiting young people into the use of illegal psychoactive drugs.

Although media attention to drugs and drug use declined between the late 1960's and late 1970's, the actual use of drugs did not. Surveys point to a strong increase during this period. The late 1970's and early 1980's probably represent another turning point in the recreational use of marijuana, hallucinogens, sedatives, and amphetamines. Recent studies show a reduction in the use of most drug types through the 1980's.

Cocaine and its derivative, crack, however, seem to be major exceptions, as their use and abuse continue to grow. Crack is a refined form of cocaine. First appearing in the mid 1980's, it rapidly became one of the most widely abused illicit drug in the United States.

New forms of older drugs continue to appear. "Ecstasy" is a methamphetamine that was first synthesized some 70 years ago as an appetite suppressant. It is a mild hallucinogen whose negative effects can be long lasting. "Ice," a methamphetamine, is as addictive as crack, but its side effects may be even more devastating.

WHY AMERICANS DETEST DRUGS AND DRUG USE

While a moral prejudice against the use of drugs probably had its roots in the 1920's, the current views against their use can be traced, in large part, to the era of the 1960's. Three broad stereotypes can be sighted that will encompass the majority of the American public during the 1960's through today. First, is group we will refer to as "Hippies". These were a significant minority of primarily adolescents. Motivated by various rock groups, such as The Beatles, The Rolling Stones, and The Who, it became fashionable to protest against what was generally referred to as The Establishment.The methods of displaying unification to this movement varied from nontraditional clothing to long hair styles.

Another popular method of protest became the widespread use of drugs, primarily, marijuana, hallucinogens, and amphetamines. A common theme among this subculture was an aversion to war. A particular target was, of course, the Vietnam war.

A second group was the actual participants in the Vietnam War. These soldiers, were in the same age group as the Hippies but circumstances landed them in Southeast Asia. Perhaps, due to the pressures associated with this war combined with the antiwar movement in the U.S., these soldiers and the hippies had a very high percentage of drug experimentation and some addiction to illegal drugs.

The third group is what we shall refer to as The Establishment. This consisted of the mainstream at that time in America. This group, likely a majority, was primarily the older generation, the parents and grandparents, the politicians, and businessmen. The Establishment was not only alarmed by the actions of the younger generation, but they also felt seriously threatened by them. These "unkempt youths" were questioning every aspect of the society that The Establishment had grown up respecting and cherishing.

Mainstream America viewed the "decadent youth" as having been corrupted. "If these youths represent our future leaders, how can we feel secure about our future?" was the question on the minds of many in The Establishment. The media was full of drug horror stories. These included the deaths of some very well known citizens from rock stars to hollywood celebrities. Many 1960's era motion pictures portrayed skewed and inaccurate pictures of the effect of drug use on an individual.

In many cases it was concluded that the drug use caused unacceptable behavior. This behavior varied from "dropping out" to suicidal tendencies. Some even concluded that drugs were a communist plot designed to subvert our youth.

The natural conclusion, drawn by the majority of the establishment group was "Drugs cause unacceptable behavior. All drug use should be abolished and all drug users are a danger to society and our belief system." The psychological collision of these three groups is the basis for the difficulty of most citizens to look rationally rather than emotionally at drug use in this country.

The very belief system of the adult Establishment had been threatened and questioned by the youth of the country. This is also one reason that any argument in favor of legalizing drugs today can amount to political suicide. Any government official with the audacity to suggest that our current methods are not working seems to be challenging the belief that drug use is bad.

Recently, the deaths of such popular figures as Len Bias, River Phoenix, and John Bellucci have been used as examples of the danger of drug use. For reasons that are not clear, the press, government officials, and most figures of authority, seem to avoid any portrayal of the positive side of drug use.

The fact must be that there are any number of positive benefits to drug use, or no one would use them. The primary benefits seem to be the temporary feeling of euphoria obtained from their use. To a lesser extent, freedom from physical, and emotional pain, and many more positive traits can be associated with drug use.

Perhaps drug use, in itself, should not be considered bad! Drug abuse is, perhaps, bad, but If **all** drug use was bad virtually every citizen in the country could be labeled as a bad citizen. Coffee, aspirin cigarettes, and alcohol are all drugs. Perhaps it is time to reevaluate our laws and our national objectives. What do we really want to accomplish? How can we best achieve our national goals?

Our war on drugs has been through many stages since the turn of the century. Over 75 years and untold billions of dollars have been spent in an attempt to eradicate drug use in the U.S. Has it been successful? Has our tremendous invest-ment been worthwhile? A look at your daily newspaper and our current prison population clearly says no.

This book examines our current drug policy and offers some viable alternatives.

Chapter

Two

> *After 20 years on the bench ,*
> *I have concluded that federal drug*
> *laws are a disaster. It is time to get the*
> *government out of drug enforcement.*
>
> Judge Whitmann Knapp
> New York Times
> May 14, 1993

CLASSIFICATION OF PSYCHOACTIVE DRUGS

It is of paramount importance that we, as a society, begin to look at drug use in America in a logical and unemotional manner. For seventy-five years this country has been inundated with a combination of truth and fiction regarding drugs, drug abuse, and drug addiction. One is best able to evaluate a given situation when he is well informed. The following information is presented in order to give a factual analysis of the descriptions and effects of the drugs in common use in this country.

Pharmacologists, who study the effects of drugs, classify psychoactive drugs according to what they do to those who take them.

WHAT IS A DRUG?

The term drug is commonly associated with substances that may be purchased legally with prescription for medical use, such as Penicillin, which is almost never abused, and Valium, which is frequently abused. Illegal substances, such as angel dust, marijuana, or cocaine, which are taken for the purpose of getting high, or intoxicated are also drugs but are deemed to have little or no medical value.

Other substances that may be purchased legally without prescription and are commonly abused include alcohol and the nicotine contained in tobacco cigarettes. Our primary focus in this analysis, however, is on a certain type of drugs, called psychoactive drugs.

Such substances legal and illegal influence or alter the workings of the mind. They affect moods, emotions, feelings, and thinking processes.

DRUG ABUSE

The term drug abuse most often refers to the use of a drug with such frequency that it causes physical or mental harm to the user or impairs social functioning. Although the term seems to imply that users abuse the drugs they take, in fact, it is themselves or others they abuse by using drugs.

Traditionally, the term drug abuse referred to the use of any drug prohibited by law, regardless of whether it was actually harmful or not. This meant that any use of marijuana, for example, even if it occurred only once in a while, would be considered abuse, while the same level of alcohol consumption would not.

This brings up the point so often sighted by those wishing a reexamination of our drug laws. Our current laws are fraught with hypocrisy. How can we continue to spend billions of dollars in trying to eradicate marijuana use, which has minimal negative impact on most users, while allowing, even encouraging, the use of alcohol and tobacco, which kill in excess of 350,000 people per year?

In 1973 the National Commission of Marijuana and Drug Abuse declared that this definition was illogical. The term abuse, the commission stated, "has no functional utility and has become no more than an arbitrary codeword for that drug which is presently considered wrong." As a result, this definition fell into disuse.

It is not always easy to determine exactly when simple drug use becomes abuse. Thus it is far easier to study who uses illegal psychoactive drugs than it is to study who abuses them.

When researchers describe patterns of drug abuse, they usually describe the more general phenomenon of drug use, whether it leads to abuse or not. The illegal use of psychoactive drugs is vast and extensive in the United States.

Some 70 million Americans age 12 and over have tried at least one or more prohibited drugs for the purpose of getting high.

The illegal drug trade represents an enormous economic enterprise. Sales of illegal drugs in the United States may have totaled $100 billion in 1986, more than the total net sales of the largest American corporation. This was more than American farmers earned from all crops combined. About 60% of the illegal drugs sold worldwide wind up in the United States.

By far the most commonly used illegal drug is marijuana. Roughly half of episodes of illegal drug use are with marijuana alone. Of all illegal drugs, marijuana is the one users are most likely to stick with and continue using. Studies sponsored by the federal government show a significant drop off in marijuana use, however, and a substantial decline in daily or near daily use throughout the 1980's. In 1985 roughly 75 percent of all Americans under the age of 26 had at least tried marijuana; in 1988, that proportion had shrunk to 56 percent.

Cocaine is the second most commonly used drug in the United States. In 1988, 13 percent of Americans aged 12 to 25 had used cocaine at least once. With cocaine, even fewer users are heavy, chronic abusers. A pattern of episodic, regular use characterizes nearly all drug use for the purpose of recreation.

Heroin is one of the least-often used of the well known drugs. It has been used at least once by fewer than 1 American in 100. This does not deny the problem of the heavy, chronic abuser of these drugs. Indeed, there are roughly a half a million heroin addicts in the United States alone.

Most people who have taken illegal drugs have done so on an experimental basis. They typically try the drug once to a dozen times and then stop.

Most regular users of illegal drugs are moderate in their use. The typical regular marijuana smoker is a casual, once in a while user. Still, a sizable minority does use the drug frequently, to the point of abuse.

DRUG DEPENDENCE

Drug abuse must be distinguished from drug dependence. Drug dependence, formerly called drug addiction, is defined by three basic characteristics. First, users continue to take a drug over an extended period of time. Just how long this period is depends on the drug and the user.

Second, users find it difficult to stop using the drug. They seem powerless to quit. Users take extraordinary and often harmful measures to continue using the drug. They will drop out of school, steal, leave their families, go to jail, and lose their jobs to keep using their drug. How dependence producing a drug is can be measured by how much users go through to continue taking it.

Third, if users stop taking their drug, if their supply of the drug is cut off, or if they are forced to quit for any reason, they will undergo painful physical or mental distress. The experience of withdrawal distress, called the withdrawal syndrome, is a sure sign that a drug is dependency producing and that a given user is dependent on a particular drug. Drug dependence may lead to drug abuse especially of illegal drugs.

TYPES OF PSYCHOACTIVE DRUGS

Psychoactive, or mind altering, substances are found the world over. The coca plant grows in the Andes of South America and contains 1 to 2 percent cocaine. The marijuana plant, Cannabis sativa, contains a group of chemicals called tetrahydrocannabinol, or THC. This plant grows wild in most countries, including the United States. The opium poppy is the source for opium, morphine, heroin, and codeine. It grows in the Middle East and the Far East. Hallucinogens (such as LSD), the amphetamines such as speed, and sedatives such as methaqualone (Quaalude, or ludes) and barbiturates, are manufactured in clandestine laboratories worldwide.

DEPRESSANTS

Depressants slow down or depress signals passing through the central nervous system and produce relaxation, and lower anxiety. At higher doses they produce drowsiness and/or sleep. They include sedatives, such as barbiturates, methaqualone, alcohol, and tranquilizers, such as Valium.

One distinct group of depressants are those which dull the mind's perception of pain. In medicine these drugs are used as painkillers, or analgesics. These drugs are called narcotics. They include heroin, morphine, opium, and codeine.

In addition to their painkilling properties, these depressants also produce a strong high and are intensely dependency producing. Some drugs cannot be placed neatly in this stimulant depressant spectrum.

ALCOHOL

Alcohol, probably the oldest drug known, has been used since the earliest societies for which records exist.

Of the numerous types of alcohol, ethyl alcohol is the type consumed in drinking. In its pure form, it is a clear substance with little odor.

People drink alcohol in three main kinds of beverages. BEERS, which are made from grain through brewing and fermentation and contain from 3% to 8% alcohol. WINES, which are fermented from fruits such as grapes and con-

36

tain from 8% to 12% alcohol naturally, and up
to 21% when fortified by adding alcohol. And
distilled beverages (spirits) such as WHISKEY,
GIN, and VODKA, which on the average contain from 40% to 50% alcohol.

**Drinkers may become addicted to any of
these beverages.**

MARIJUANA

Marijuana (also spelled marihuana) is the common name given to any drug preparation from
the hemp plant, Cannabis sativa. Various forms
of this drug are known by different names
throughout the world, such as kif in Morocco,
dagga in South Africa, and ganja in India.
Hashish refers to a dried, resinous substance
that exudes from the flowering tops of the
plant.

In Western culture, cannabis preparations have
acquired a variety of slang names, including
grass, pot, tea, reefer, weed, and Mary Jane.

Cannabis has been smoked, eaten in cakes, and
drunk in beverages. In Western cultures
marijuana is prepared most often as a tobacco-
like mixture that is smoked in a pipe or rolled
into a cigarette.

One of the oldest known drugs, cannabis was
acknowledged as early as 2700 B.C., in a
Chinese manuscript. Throughout the centuries
it has been used both medicinally and as an
intoxicant. The major psychoactive component
of this drug, however, was not identified until
the mid 1960's; this ingredient is
tetrahydrocannabinol, commonly known as
THC.

At present, other cannabinoids have been isolated and their possible biochemical activities are being explored. Psychoactive compounds are found in all parts of the male and female plant, with the greatest concentration in the flowering tops. The content of these active compounds varies greatly from plant to plant, depending on genetic and environmental factors.

Marijuana has its major physiological effects on the cardiovascular and central nervous systems. These effects are primarily sedative and hallucinogenic. Low doses psychologically produce a sense of well-being, relaxation, and sleepiness. Higher doses cause mild sensory distortions, altered time sense, loss of short term memory, loss of balance, and difficulty in completing thought processes. Even higher doses can result in feelings of depersonalization, severe anxiety and panic, and a toxic psychosis. Hallucinations, loss of insight, delusions, and paranoia are also associated with chronic use.

Physiologically, the heart rate increases and blood vessels of the eye dilate, causing reddening. A feeling of tightness in the chest and a lack of muscular coordination may also occur.

Research suggests that marijuana smoke may have a longterm harmful effect on the lungs. Users may develop tolerance for the drug, but studies have not determined whether physical dependence results.

The use of marijuana as an intoxicant in the United States became a problem of public concern in the 1930's. Regulatory laws were passed in 1937, and criminal penalties were instituted for possession and sale of the botanical drug. In 1968 the possession and sale of THC, the psychoactive chemical component, was restricted to research. Despite these measures, marijuana continued to be widely used in later decades as various groups sought to decriminalize its possession.

A survey in the late 1970's indicated that at least 43 million Americans had tried the drug. In the 1980's, however, surveys of high school and college students showed that marijuana use was steadily declining. The number of high school seniors for instance, who had tried the drug decreased from 50.8 percent in 1979 to 33.1 percent in 1989.

Conversely, cultivation of marijuana in the United States is increasing, accounting for 25 percent of the U.S. domestic market by 1990. Moreover, new growing practices have increased the potency (THC content) of domestically produced marijuana five fold or more, causing concern among drug abuse experts about adverse effects from higher THC doses.

Medically, marijuana and THC preparations are sometimes used to treat glaucoma, because they help to reduce pressure within the eye. In 1985 the Food and Drug Administration also approved the use of synthetic THC (dronabinol) for treating the nausea and vomiting that can accompany cancer chemotherapy.

HALLUCINOGENS

Hallucinogens include LSD, mescaline, and psilocybin. They produce unusual mental states, such as psychedelic visions. Hallucinogens, a class of Psychotropic Drugs, are a group of plant derived or synthetically produced chemical substances. Human beings have used many of these materials, throughout history, to modify their state of consciousness for medicinal, religious, or recreational purposes.

The most potent hallucinogen is LSD (lysergic acid diethylamide), often simply called "acid." Other hallucinogens are mescaline and psilocybin; the marijuana plant and its derivative hashish are considered mild hallucinogens.

In the United States, federal law currently prohibits the manufacture, distribution, or possession of hallucinogenic drugs except for research approved by the government.

SOURCES OF HALLUCINOGENS

Several plants are still used for their psychedelic properties by indigenous peoples worldwide, especially on the American continents. Many such plants are used as sacraments, in magic medicine, and in divination rites by native shamans, healers, witch doctors, and herbalists. The knowledge and use of these plants, regarded as sacred or magic beings that communicate directly with the user, have been handed down for centuries through traditions intimately connected with religion.

Hallucinogens occur in plants of distant botanical families. One of these plants is the desert cactus, Lophophora williamsii, known in Spanish as peyote, from which mescaline is derived. Peyote buttons, the crowns of the cacti, are used today by the Yaqui, Tarahumara, and Huichol Indians.

The tribes of the Mexican highlands use several species of sacred mushrooms, which contain psilocybin (an alkaloid), belonging to the genus Psilocybe. They were called teonanacatl ("God's flesh") by the ancient Nahuatl Indians. Tribes in the Amazonian jungles of South America inhale a preparation of the leguminous epena (Piptadenia peregrina and Virola calophylla), which contain dimethyltryptamine, a short action, intense hallucinogenic alkaloid.

LSD is made from a mixture of diethylamide and the alkaloid lysergic acid, found in the seeds of the morning glory flower, which, when ingested, produces some mild psychedelic effects.

Hashish is a resinous extract from the female hemp plant, Cannabis sativa, which is also the source of marijuana (usually classified as a minor psychedelic agent or a cognodysleptic).

EFFECTS OF HALLUCINOGENS

The initial effects induced by the ingestion of a moderate dose of a hallucinogen are lightheadedness, a sense of wellbeing, and increased attention to perceptions, sensations, and inner mental events. Perceptual modifications follow. They are initially manifested as vivid visual imagery that then evolves to illusions and finally to hallucinations. Emotions are intensified and may include euphoria, apathy, serenity, or anxiety.

In later stages, following a large dose, a person may experience a feeling of union with nature associated with a dissolution of personal identity; a dissociative reaction, in which the subject loses contact with immediate reality, may also occur. Such sensations could lead to terror or panic, but the experience is determined by the person's mental state, the structure of his or her personality, the physical setting, and cultural influences.

The role of culture and belief systems is in fact primary in the modulation of hallucinogenic states. The experience following the ingestion of a hallucinogenic drug is sometimes called a "trip," termed good or bad depending on its effects on the user. The effects may last for several hours or days and may recur. Occasionally the effects may resemble some symptoms of schizophrenia, and sometimes the hallucinogen precipitates toxic psychotic reactions.

AMPHETAMINES AND STIMULANTS

Stimulants are defined as, "Drugs that speed up signals passing through the nervous system, comprised of the brain and spinal cord, and produce alertness and arousal." Higher doses cause excitability, and inhibit fatigue and sleep. They include the amphetamines, cocaine, caffeine, and nicotine.

Some stimulants also impair appetite and may be prescribed medically to obese people in order to promote weight loss. Most users of these drugs experience a sense of well being (euphoria). But this reaction depends greatly on the drug taken and the dose. Signs of over-stimulation by these drugs, such as muscle tremors or irregular heart rate, are common.

Almost all societies have discovered some indigenous plant that produces stimulant effects. Coca leaves, for instance, are chewed by South American Indians and are the source of the drug cocaine. That leaves, whose active ingredient is norpseudoephedrine, are chewed by Middle Eastern peoples. Betel nuts, containing arecoline, are chewed by Asians and South Pacific Islanders. Cocaine and caffeine are the most familiar natural stimulants, and the amphetamines the best known synthetic ones.

The antidepressants are sometimes classified as stimulants, as is nicotine. But nicotine functions as both a stimulant and a depressant. Other drugs that have been used as emergency stimulants include Strychnine, Pentylenetetrazol, and ammonia.

Amphetamines, widely used in medical practice until recently, are sympathomimetic stimulants. That is, they act physiologically in ways similar to the sympathetic nervous system. Although synthetic, they are chemically related to ephedrine, a drug derived from a Chinese shrub, Ephedra dystocia, which is a mild stimulant used to alleviate respiratory ailments. Amphetamines are known as "pep pills" or "diet pills" because they increase energy and feelings of euphoria and decrease the desire for food.

Amphetamine (phenylisopropylamine) was first introduced into medical practice in the 1930's. It was widely used as an appetite suppressant, as a treatment for narcolepsy (uncontrollable attacks of sleepiness), and as a treatment for hyperactive children. A curious reverse effect has been observed and stimulants actually seem to relax overactive children. Amphetamine was also occasionally inhaled as a nasal decongestant.

Other drugs with similar actions were also synthesized, including methamphetamine, methylphenidate, and pipradol.

Soon after the introduction of amphetamine-related drugs in medicine, however, people discovered their euphoriant effect and began to abuse them. In the years immediately following World War II, for instance, the Japanese government made enormous amounts of amphetamines available to its armed forces. They were used during wartime to prevent sleepiness and to keep the troops alert. Japan subsequently had a major outbreak of amphetamine abuse, especially among young people.

Abuse of this stimulant remained a relatively minor problem in the United States until the enormous upsurge of drug abuse in the 1960's. The drug methamphetamine, for example, known in street terminology as "speed," became a favored drug because it could be manufactured more easily by illicit means than could other, related drugs. Speed can be manufactured in a garage with a minimum of cost and effort, thereby making enforcement difficult or impossible.

The drug diethyproprion was synthesized to alter amphetamines in chemical structure and reduce its euphoriant effect. But the potential for abuse was not eliminated. This applies, as well, to other amphetamine related drugs in common use for weight loss. Such drugs, which are known as anorexics or anorectics, include benzphetamine, chlorphentermine, phen-metrazine, phendimetrazine, and phenter-mopine, among others.

Tolerance develops with chronic use, so that doses up to 1,000 times those used medically are employed by drug abusers. Such abuse, however, cannot be sustained. The user, when forced to stop, has such withdrawal symptoms as excessive sleepiness, ravenous appetite, and mental depression. Long term psychological changes may also follow.

Because of the dangers associated with the abuse of stimulants, their medical indications and manufacture have been severely curtailed in a number of countries. Although these measures have resulted in the decline of am-phetamine use, this reduction has been paral-leled by an increase in the illegal use of cocaine.

CAFFEINE

The beverages coffee, tea, cocoa, and many soft drinks contain caffeine, the most widely used stimulant drug in the world. Cocoa contains not only caffeine but also theobromine, a com-pound closely related to caffeine. Similarly, tea contains caffeine and theophylline, a stimulant drug often used medically to alleviate asthma. Cola drinks derive their caffeine content (2 per-cent) from the kola nut, which was chewed by people of the Sudan for its stimulant effects. Few people who drink coffee, tea, cocoa, or cola-flavored soft drinks consider themselves drug users, because these beverages are ac-cepted socially and because the amount of caf-feine is small.

A moderately strong cup of coffee may contain about 75 to 125 mg of caffeine, a dose that, for most persons, is just above the threshold for recognition. Furthermore, people differ greatly in their susceptibility to the stimulant effects of this drug, a difference thought to be based on genetic factors.

Even over the course of an individual's lifetime, the response to caffeine may change. With increasing age caffeine users may experience for the first time insomnia or palpitations of the heart associated with irregular beats. Heavy users often become nervous, irritable, apprehensive, restless, and unable to sleep. Such symptoms may be construed as a psychiatric disorder unless the history of caffeine misuse is known. Recognition of the drug effects of these beverages has led to the increased use of decaffeinated coffee.

COCAINE

Cocaine, an alkaloid drug found in the leaves of the coca plant, was first used medically in 1884 by Carl Koller, an Austrian ophthalmologic surgeon. Because of its effectiveness in depressing nerve endings, its chief medical use has been as a local anesthetic, especially for the nose, throat, and cornea. It has been largely replaced by less toxic, synthetic local anesthetics. Used systemically, cocaine stimulates the central nervous system, producing feelings of excitation, elation, well being, enhanced physical strength and mental capacity, and a lessened sense of fatigue. It also causes increased heart rate, blood pressure, and temperature; in large doses, it can cause death.

Those who abuse cocaine because of its stimulating effects frequently do so by sniffing its fine white powder, often called "snow."

Cocaine is psychologically habit forming. Abrupt cessation of use of the drug, or withdrawal, is followed by hunger, fatigue, and depression.

Sigmund Freud was among the first to describe the effect of cocaine, on the central nervous system. He confirmed the euphoric effects and the increased energy and alertness noted by coca leaf chewers for centuries. Once cocaine was isolated (1855), it came into medical use as a local anesthetic and as a nasal decongestant, because it shrinks mucous membranes. Its role in medicine has declined, but it has since become a major drug of abuse. Smoked, sniffed, or injected, cocaine produces a short-term sense of intense euphoria and alertness, but the drug is debilitating and may lead to strong psychological addiction.

Long term abuse can damage the nasal septum, cause skin abscesses, and lead to psychoses. Overdoses of the drug are occasionally fatal.

CRACK COCAINE

In the mid 1980's the use of "crack," a new, relatively inexpensive form of cocaine, emerged and spread rapidly. Crack is highly concentrated chemically reconstituted cocaine, in a pebble shape, which is smoked. By 1990, the use of the highly addictive crack was widespread in the United States and had become a national issue.

A principal cause of concern was the increase in the rates of violent crime in the deteriorated urban areas in which crack dealers were active. Crack also bore much responsibility for such social ills as addicted newborns and child abuse. The chronic user can develop a full toxic paranoid psychosis, which can lead to violent antisocial behavior. Long term use can also result in weight loss, deterioration of the nervous system, and digestive problems.

Crack cocaine is much more addictive than cocaine, and is normally smoked. This drug has received a great deal of press recently as a result of its strongly addictive traits. Its popularity seems to stem from the quality of the effect of the drug coupled with a relatively inexpensive cost per usage.

The fact that increased use will be required as a result of the eventual addiction does not seem to be a deterrent.

With this drug, as with most other addictive drugs, addiction seems to be the exception to the rule. **While crack may be among the most addictive drugs known to man, indications are that only 3 to 4 percent of users become addicted and remain so for long periods of time.**

Chapter

Three

CURRENT METHODS OF DISTRIBUTION, LAW ENFORCEMENT, AND TREATMENT

CURRENT DRUG TRAFFICKING METHODS

Drug trafficking refers to the illegal manufacture or sale, or both, of controlled substances. These range from drugs having a high potential for drug abuse and no generally accepted medical use (heroin, for example) to those having an accepted medical use but that can lead to dependence (phenobarbital, for example).

The international trafficking of drugs consists of an elaborate network, often involving "official" protection and organized crime. Many drugs enter the United States through illegal channels. For example, a high grade variety of marijuana grown in Thailand is shipped across the Pacific on great circular routes before approaching the West Coast for distribution. Much of the cocaine brought into the country from South America enters through Florida and is driven to the West Coast before being distributed to dealers.

HEROIN is a chemical derivative of opium. Juice of the poppy is cultivated in the Middle East, Asia, and Mexico by a number of organizations. In the Golden Triangle of Southeast Asia, which includes parts of Laos, Thailand, and Burma, The Shan United Army maintains an impressive military presence supported by trafficking in opium. A second major group consists of remnants of the defeated Chinese Nationalist Army, which maintains itself by recruiting local tribesmen and dealing in opium. A third group is the Burmese Communist party, whose military forces turned to drug trafficking when their former patron, the People's Republic of China, cut off aid.

OPIUM is also cultivated by Pathan tribesmen in Afghanistan and by "crime families" in Mexico. The poppies produce opium gum, which is converted into base morphine and finally heroin. It is then smuggled into Europe and the United States at a purity level of more than 90%. Smuggling is accomplished by couriers for a variety of international organized crime groups, Chinese triads, Italian Mafia, and Comoro groups and by independents. After importation the heroin is diluted to a purity level of about 5%. Street sale to addicts is carried on by numerous groups, particularly street gangs in urban areas.

COCAINE is derived from the coca plant, grown in such Latin American countries as Bolivia (where it is legal), Brazil, Colombia, Ecuador, and Peru. Coca is usually grown in remote areas where government control is tenuous. Coca is often a very significant local cash crop, and attempts to suppress trafficking fans anti-government sentiment in countries beset by revolutionary groups. This fact, combined with government inefficiency and outright corruption, makes coca growing difficult to eradicate. Much of the cocaine entering the

United States arrives via Colombia, where sophisticated, powerful, and violent criminal organizations like the "Medellin cartel" maintain elaborate drug networks.

Efforts to contain this extraordinarily profitable drug trafficking have proven ineffective. Attempts are thwarted by corruption, even at very high levels, and the law of "supply and demand."

Profits are tremendous. When a kilo of base morphine, for example, purchased overseas for about $15,000, reaches the U.S. it has a street value of about $2 million.

Successful interceptions merely drive up the price and create a vacuum that traffickers rush to fill.

The Medellin Cartel, for example, has been considered the largest and most powerful distributor of cocaine for many years.

Recent efforts to eradicate this cartel, resulted in the capturing, imprisoning, and death of many of its most powerful leaders.

Did the recent death of Paublo Escobar, the undisputed king pin of the Medellin Cartel, solve the cocaine problem in the U.S.? Hardly.

Prior to his death, Mr. Escobar had amassed a $4 billion fortune. It is little wonder that he was difficult to apprehend and imprison. In a poor country like Columbia, a little bit of bribery goes a long way toward insuring the cooperation of key people. The big mistake that Escobar made was his ruthless behavior. During his reign as a drug lord he was alleged to have arranged the murder of over 115 Columbian federal judges. He also had a reputation for eliminating anyone who crossed him. He eventually murdered with such impunity, and in so brazen a fashion that public opinion demanded his incarceration. Escobar agreed to spend a short sentence in a prison that he had custom built to his own specifications.

Before the world knew that the Medellin Cartel and Paublo Escobar were being seriously pursued by Columbian authorities, a newer, and much more powerful Cartel was being organized in nearby Cali, Columbia and is now referred to as the Cali Cartel.

These newer "high tech" drug lords are extremely sophisticated with cellular phones FAX machines, computerized order processing and so forth. They have learned from the mistakes of Paublo Escobar, and keep a much lower profile. They are considered by most to be virtually invincible, as they have nearly every person for miles around on their payroll. Any attempt by the Columbian government to invade the homes or factories owned by this cartel is defeated before it begins.

The point is that supply and demand always works. If we manage to cut off the supply of a product in one location or country a new, often more efficient, distribution center will soon fill in the gap.

U.S. Citizens, alarmed by escalating usage, declared a "war on drugs" during the Reagan administration. Any informed citizen knows that we have spent billions of dollars on this effort and have made no headway whatever during the 13 years of this war. We have more drug use in this country than ever before.

DRUG LAW ENFORCEMENT

In 1970 the U.S. Congress passed the Comprehensive Drug Abuse Prevention and Control Act. Most of the states followed suit by basing their state legislation on the federal model. The Control Act distinguishes among several categories of drugs based on their abuse potential and their medical utility.

Drugs that supposedly have a high potential for abuse and no currently accepted medical use, including heroin, LSD, hallucinogens, and marijuana, may be used legally only in a federally approved scientific research experiment. Because of their high abuse potential, these drugs are tightly controlled by federal and state laws.

While the laws are strict, enforcement is nearly impossible due to widespread drug use and availability through underground sources.

Such drugs as morphine, cocaine, methaqualone, the amphetamines, and short acting barbiturates are also regarded as having great abuse potential, although they do have accepted medical use.

Rigid prescription procedures are employed to maintain tight controls over their use, but again enforcement has little effect on limiting use.

Such medically prescribed drugs as long-acting barbiturates and non-narcotic painkillers are considered to have a lesser abuse potential, although they may lead to some physical or psychological dependence. These drugs have more relaxed controls. Tranquilizers, such as Valium, are classified as having low abuse potential.

There has been a remarkable drop in the number of prescriptions written for psychoactive drugs from the 1970's to the 1980's. In the 1980's the prescription use of the short acting barbiturates, for example, was only a quarter of what it was in the early 1970's. The prescription use of the amphetamines dropped by over half during this same period.

Many other countries have also placed severe restrictions on the prescribing of drugs by doctors and have thus greatly reduced the frequency of amphetamine abuse. In Canada, Australia, and most Scandinavian countries, amphetamines are banned from use in medicine except in rare cases.

While restricting psychoactive pharmaceuticals has brought about a reduction in the number of legal prescriptions written for them, the picture for illegal street drugs is far more complicated.

The illicit use of barbiturates and other sedatives, methaqualone, and tranquilizers dropped significantly only between the early to the mid-1980's. This lagged behind a decline in their legal prescription use by at least half a decade. The illegal use of stimulants, however, at least in the high schools may be as high as it was a decade ago. The demand for drugs for illegal purposes remains high in spite of law enforcement efforts. For example, between 1970 and 1977, the number of arrests on marijuana charges in the United States more than doubled, from 188,000 to 457,000. During this same period, however, the percentage of the American population who had ever used marijuana also doubled for most age categories. **Arrest did not seem to deter marijuana use.**

Likewise, the number of arrests on the charge of narcotics possession and sale increased from 533,000 in 1980 to over 850,000 in 1988. The use of heroin and the other narcotics remained steady during this period, while the use of cocaine exploded.

In the face of mounting public concern, Congress passed strong new drug laws and enforcement measures, along with treatment and education programs in 1986.

The United States is only one among many countries with a drug problem. Drug production and trade are of primary concern to the governments of Pakistan, Burma, Thailand, and Laos (the so called golden triangle countries). India is one of the largest producers and users of opium. Mexico, Egypt, and Morocco are the primary producers of marijuana and its derivatives. South America is the primary supplier of cocaine and crack cocaine.

In an effort to control the international flow of illicit drugs, the United States has entered into several agreements with European and Asian nations to share intelligence and coordinate law enforcement activities.

Federal efforts to reduce the trafficking of narcotics in the United States have called for the establishment of several regional task forces.

The effort to stem the use of illicit drugs in the United States
and the related cost has escalated dramatically over the last three decades, Unfortunately we have seen little or no reduction in usage.

Many people feel it is time to rethink our position and to begin dealing realistically with this chronic, and debilitating problem.

FEDERAL LAW & DRUG TESTING IN THE WORKPLACE

Let's examine some of the costly efforts, currently in place, designed to eradicate drug and alcohol abuse in the workplace. These are examples of the ever-escalating number of laws, requirements, and restrictions placed on every citizen in the country, in order to attempt to control a minority of drug users.

The Drug-Free Workplace Act of 1988, has been in effect since March 1989. The law toughens federal criminal statutes and authorizes substantial funding for drug education, treatment and prevention programs. It also requires federal contractors and federal grant recipients to implement and administer a program for maintaining a drug-free workplace.

Specifically, the law requires federal grant recipients and all employers with federal contracts of $25,000 or more to certify that they will provide a drug-free workplace by fulfilling the following requirements of the law:

1. Publishing a statement informing employees that the unlawful manufacture, distribution, dispensation, provision or use of controlled substances is prohibited in the workplace and

specifying what actions will be taken against employees for violating the prohibition.

2. Providing all employees involved in the performance of the contract or grant with a copy of this statement.

3. Establishing a drug-free awareness program that informs employees about the dangers of drug abuse; the availability of drug counseling, rehabilitation and employee assistance plans; the employer's policy of maintaining a drug-free workplace; and the penalties that may be assessed for drug abuse violations.

4. Notifying employees in the statement described above that, as a condition of employment on the federal contract or grant project, each employee must abide by the terms of the statement and must notify the employer of any criminal drug statute conviction for a violation occurring in the workplace not less than five days after the conviction.

5. Notifying the agency with which the employer has the contract or grant of any such conviction within ten days after being notified by an employee or by any other party.

6. Imposing a sanction on the convicted employee, up to and including termination, or requiring such employee to participate satisfactorily in a drug rehabilitation or drug abuse assistance program.

7. Making a good-faith effort to maintain a drug-free workplace by implementing the requirements set forth in the Drug-Free Workplace Act.

Employers covered by the law are subject to suspension of payments, termination of the contract or grant, suspension or debarment if the head of the contracting or granting organization determines that the employer has made a false certification to the agency, has failed to fulfill the requirements of the law or has an excessive number of employees convicted of drug violations occurring in the workplace, thus indicating that efforts to provide a drug-free workplace have failed.

Employers who are debarred are ineligible for other federal contracts or grants for up to five years.

DOT Regulations. The U.S. Department of Transportation's (DOT's) final interim rule on drug testing regulations became effective in December 1988. The regulations cover several occupations under DOT jurisdiction, including mass transit workers, natural gas and pipeline workers, motor carrier workers, aviation workers and railroad workers.

Employers with transportation positions covered by DOT must test job applicants as well as employees, during routine physicals, on a random basis, upon reasonable cause, and after accidents.

Employers must test for marijuana, cocaine, opiates, amphetamines and phencyclidine (PCP). Testing for alcohol or substances other than those listed above is not allowed under the regulations unless the employer obtains authorization from the appropriate DOT agency. In addition, specimens collected for testing cannot be used to perform any other test or analysis not specifically authorized by the DOT agency.

Employers subject to DOT jurisdiction must follow set procedures for conducting any form of drug testing on the urine sample of any applicant or employee required to be tested under DOT's regulations. Among these procedures are the following:

1. A mandatory "urine custody and control form" must be used to document the collection and shipment of a specimen.

2. Measures must be taken at the specimen collection site to protect the privacy of the employee or applicant being tested and the integrity of the specimen provided.

3. All laboratories performing the tests should be certified by the U.S. Department of Health and Human Services, should have qualified and responsible personnel, should perform the specimen analysis in a secure and reliable manner, and should adhere to quality control and quality assurance standards.

4. A final review of all test results should be conducted by a medical review officer, who is a licensed physician trained to interpret and evaluate positive test results and who is knowledgeable about substance abuse disorders.

The regulations also deal with the confidentiality of test results and with employee access to records relevant to drug tests and certification reviews of the laboratory that processed the tests. Because each DOT operating administration has variations on several standard regulations, any employer that falls under one of their jurisdictions must learn about these variations and accommodate them. The operating administrations are the Federal Highway Administration, the Federal Aviation Administration and the Urban Mass Transit Administration.

DOD Interim Rules. Under the U.S. Department of Defense's (DOD's) interim rules, which went into effect in January 1989, all defense contracts must contain a clause requiring a drug-free workplace whenever the work involved (1) entails access to classified information, (2) bears on national security concerns in some other way or (3) necessitates protecting the health and safety of those using—or affected by—the product or performance of the contract.

The drug-free workplace clause requires the DOD contractor to take the following actions:

1. Implement employee assistance programs.

2. Implement supervisory training programs to help identify and address illegal drug use by employees.

3. Provide for self-referrals and supervisory referrals for treatment.

4. Identify illegal drug use. This is to be done with the help of testing on a controlled and carefully monitored basis.

5. Establish a drug testing program, including random testing, for employees in sensitive positions (that is, those with access to classified information or in positions involving national

security, health or safety, or requiring a high degree of trust and confidence).

At their discretion, employers covered by the DOD clause can establish a drug testing program for employees in non-sensitive positions when there is a reasonable suspicion that illegal drugs are being used, after an accident or other unsafe practice, as a follow-up to drug counseling or rehabilitation, and when employees volunteer to be tested. The clause also permits contractors to test job applicants for illegal drug use. In addition, the DOD clause requires contractors to adopt procedures to deal with employees found to be abusing drugs (including the removal of employees in sensitive positions found to use illegal drugs until the employer believes the workers are capable of handling those jobs).

It is important to note that the provisions of the DOD contract clause relating to testing do not apply if they conflict with any state or local laws or with an existing collective bargaining agreement. However, parts of the clause that conflict with a labor agreement are to be raised at the next negotiating session, when employers are expected to make a "concerted effort" to ensure that the new agreement complies with the DOD clause
.

The cost of a DOD contractor's drug programs may be charged to the contract in accordance with the federal acquisition regulations.

The Vocational Rehabilitation Act of 1973 defines drug abuse as a protected handicap and prohibits employers who receive federal funds from discriminating in hiring, firing or other practices involving employees with protected handicaps.

However, since the act's amendment in 1978, individuals whose abuse of drugs or alcohol interferes with the performance of their duties, or is a threat to the safety or property of others, are exempt from this protection. Hence, to be protected by this law, employees must show that they are handicapped by their drug or alcohol addiction, but not so handicapped that they have trouble performing their jobs or pose threats to others.

How many ludicrous laws, like the one above, must we pass before we realize that we are fighting a war we cannot win?

The Americans with Disabilities Act of 1990, prohibits discrimination against "qualified people with disabilities" and severely limits an employer's ability to inquire into an employee's or job applicant's medical history. It does, however, permit drug testing and does not bar employers from prohibiting alcohol or illegal drug use in the workplace.

Although the act does not protect current illegal substance abusers and alcoholics who cannot safely perform their jobs, it does protect those who have been rehabilitated, who are participating in a supervised rehabilitation program and not currently using drugs, or who are erroneously regarded as engaging in the use of illegal drugs.

For employers with 25 or more workers, the act became effective June 26, 1992; for employers with 15 or more workers it becomes effective on July 26,1994.

Nuclear Regulatory Commission, Defense and Transportation Department drug standards will continue to apply to employees those specific industries.

Collective Bargaining Obligations. The National Labor Relations Act requires unionized employers to bargain about terms and conditions of employment, a category that includes drug testing and the requirement that workers be "drug free." This means that before implementing a drug-free workplace policy, unionized employers must notify their union representatives of what they intend to do and bargain in good faith, either until an agreement is reached or until an impasse is declared.

In two June 1989 rulings, the National Labor Relations Board (NLRB) determined that although employers must bargain prior to establishing drug and alcohol testing programs for current employees, this obligation does not extend to drug testing of job applicants.

In Johnson-Bateman, the NLRB held that testing current employees is a mandatory subject of bargaining under the Taft Hartley Act because it affects the "terms and conditions" of employment subject to negotiation under the act. Like mandatory polygraph tests or physical examinations, drug and alcohol testing is "plainly germane to the working environment" and does not involve matters "at the core of entrepreneurial control" reserved to management, the NLRB stated.

The International Brotherhood of Electrical Workers has taken Florida Power & Light Co. (FPL) to court over stricter drug testing measures imposed on some 4,000 FPL nuclear workers and contractors. The new policy increases the frequency of random tests tenfold and introduces more severe penalties, up to and including immediate dismissal. The union charges that the policy exceeds federal guidelines. The U.S. Nuclear Regulatory Commission requires only that nuclear power employees who test positive be removed from the job site and counseled for 14 days. The Commission says it regards its standards as minimums only. FPL says it intends to continue to provide treatment for drug users who come forward voluntarily.

With respect to employers in the railroad and airline industries, the Supreme Court has held that requiring drug testing as part of a routine physical examination was implied under Conrail's collective bargaining agreement and therefore constituted a "minor dispute". In other words, Conrail had the discretion to include drug testing in all physical examinations. The court also concluded that the purpose of the testing was not necessarily disciplinary, but medical.

Other Relevant Federal Law. Employers looking for ways to detect workplace substance abuse or drug dealing should be aware that the **Federal Omnibus Control and Safe Streets Act of 1968** restricts all employers' use of electronic eavesdropping devices to intercept employees' conversations. Federal statutes also prohibit most employers from conducting polygraph examinations on applicants and employees. Visual surveillance (which includes the use of closed-circuit television) is generally permissible as long as the surveillance is not used where employees have reasonable expectations of privacy (such as in restrooms).

Employers should also be aware that the Food and Drug Administration held on June 13,1990, that commercial and radioimmunoassay drug-screening tests using hair samples are not reliable or scientifically sound for use in the workplace, and that the testing procedures involved in radioimmunoassay hair tests violate the federal Food, Drug and Cosmetic Act.

Constitutional Considerations. With respect to public sector employers, the implementation of drug policies, including requiring public employees to take drug tests, is regulated by the Fourth Amendment's restriction against unreasonable searches and seizures. Accordingly, blood tests, breathalyzers and urinalysis tests have all been held to be searches regulated by the Fourth Amendment.

Generally, a drug test policy will be deemed reasonable if the employer has individualized, reasonable suspicion that an employee is involved with drugs prior to testing the employee. Such individualized suspicion includes, but is not limited to, the employee's involvement in a work-related accident, an unexplained decline in the employee's performance, an unexplained increase in absenteeism or observable characteristics of substance abuse such as slurred speech, staggering or the presence of drugs or drug paraphernalia.

Absent such individualized suspicion, most courts have found drug testing programs to violate the Fourth Amendment.

However, the U.S. Supreme Court has recently ruled that individual suspicion is not needed where the employee has a diminished expectation of privacy because the industry in which the employee works is highly regulated by the government or involves issues of national security or safety.

Even a valid drug testing policy may violate the privacy rights of employees if it is conducted in an overly intrusive manner. For example, mass drug testing of police officers was deemed too intrusive. Officers were required to give urine samples under the surveillance of test personnel and there was no evidence of any drug problem in the police force. Where the employer has documented a past drug problem among employees, however, surveillance of urine samples has been found to be permissible.

With respect to pre employment drug testing, the courts have held that such drug testing is subject to the same reasonable search and seizure restrictions as active employment testing.

Public employers' drug policies have also been challenged under Fifth and Fourteenth Amendment rights to due process. Specifically, an employee's due process rights are violated if an employer takes action based on unreliable or inaccurate drug test results. A drug test procedure will be reliable and accurate where safeguards are provided to obtain an unadulterated bodily fluid sample, chain of custody precautions are taken and a confirmatory test is performed, among other safeguards.

Pending Legislation for Private Industry. The Senate Committee on Labor and Human Resources is reviewing legislation that would set federal drug testing standards for private industry. **The Quality Assurance in the**

Private Sector Drug Testing Act of 1989 (SB 1903), sponsored by Senators. David Boren (D-OK) and Orrin Hatch (R-UT), would give private sector employers the right to conduct drug and alcohol tests on job applicants and on employees during annual physicals or during drug and alcohol rehabilitation. Random testing would be allowed only for employees in sensitive positions such as those in national security or health and safety.

The bill's supporters believe it would eliminate court challenges, but detractors argue that its provisions would invade employee rights.

Drinking on the job is a social and economic problem with a long history. With the growing popularity of illegal drugs in the 1960's and 1970's, it was to be expected that their use in the workplace would emerge as a major issue by the 1980's.

Estimates of employee drug use vary greatly, ranging from 10 percent to 25 percent. The proportion of workers who use drugs occasionally on the job has been documented, but to what extent should this concern the employer, and at what cost?

In 1986, President Reagan's Commission on Organized Crime recommended that all U.S. companies routinely test their employees for drug use. The question of drug testing has become a major issue in American politics.

Conservatives contend that the danger of drugs on the job is so great that everyone should be tested. Workers caught with traces of drugs in their bloodstream or urine should be fired or treated. In this way, they say, the incidence of drug use can be substantially reduced. Conservatives argue that the U.S. Constitution does not guarantee a pilot, for example, the right to risk the lives of hundreds of passengers.

Liberals insist that the risk to individual rights (particularly to the freedom from unreasonable search guaranteed by the 4th Amendment) posed by indiscriminate and random testing makes the program unacceptable. The government has no right, they say, to invade the workplace and monitor the bodies of workers for the presence of drugs. Some drugs leave traces in the bloodstream for weeks after use. Moreover, the tests are not completely accurate or reliable.

Some companies and government agencies have instituted drug testing programs for their employees. Drug testing is commonplace in the armed forces and is often cited as a major factor in reducing the use of drugs among military personnel.

Nonetheless, the practice of testing will never become universal for at least two reasons. First, with most jobs, an intoxicated worker is no more dangerous than a worker who is not under the influence, because the jobs themselves involve no hazard. Workers resent the intrusion of testing, particularly random testing. Although the U.S. Supreme Court ruled (1989) that the federal government could require drug testing of both private and government employees whose work involved public safety or law enforcement, the question of the constitutionality of the random testing of most workers still remains. In addition, depending on the type of test used, a single urine test for the presence of drugs may cost $250 or more, a cost that would seem to prohibit large-scale testing programs.

Despite these and other efforts, and the tremendous costs associated with compliance, little reduction in drug usage has been accomplished.

CURRENT TREATMENT METHODS

From the 1920's until the 1960's, treatment of drug abuse in the United States was practically nonexistent. During this period many officials did not believe that treatment was effective or necessary. The prevailing policy was punitive. Drug abusers and sellers were simply arrested and imprisoned, this theoretically, discouraged use. The dramatic explosion in the use and abuse of a wide range of different drugs during the 1960's demonstrated the weakness of this theory.

As a result, two treatment programs were developed during the 1960's. They were aimed mainly at narcotic, especially heroin, addiction. These programs are Methadone Maintenance and Treatment Groups.

METHADONE

Methadone is a synthetic narcotic and is used to combat narcotic addiction. Methadone is also addictive. The purpose of the program is to administer methadone to heroin addicts in a controlled setting, such as a hospital or a clinic. The drug is taken orally, usually dissolved in artificial orange juice. Taken this way, the addict does not get high. In addition, methadone blocks the action of narcotic drugs so that addicts cannot become high, even if they were to inject heroin.

As a consequence, according to this treatment program's rationale, addicts will stop taking heroin. Although they will still be addicted to methadone, they can live a normal life, since their supply of methadone is steady and secure. There are no impurities in what they take, they only have to take methadone once a day, because it is a very slow acting drug, and they do not get high. Because the program is inexpensive to administer, methadone has become a very popular form of treatment.

Early studies on the effectiveness of the methadone treatment program were optimistic, showing a success, or cure, rate of more than 90 percent. These studies were flawed, however. Program directors had purposely selected addicts who were highly motivated to do well in the program; they had selected older addicts, many of whom discontinue narcotic addiction even without entering a treatment program; and they had not included in their results many of the patients who had dropped out of the program and returned to a life of addiction on the street.

Later, more careful studies have shown that methadone maintenance is not the cure all it was once thought to be. Improvement in the lives of addicts in the program tends to be very modest, and most addicts show little or no improvement at all. Addicts often use methadone programs to tide themselves over when heroin is difficult to obtain on the street.

TREATMENT GROUPS

Unlike Methadone Maintenance, Treatment Groups, such as Daytop Village in New York and Walden House in San Francisco, advocate a completely drug and alcohol free existence. Addicts in treatment groups are live-in residents of the program. Most of the administrators in these communities are ex-addicts, who can best understand the thinking of the addict residents. The view of these organizations is that the addict is an immature, emotionally disturbed individual who uses drugs as a crutch.

They attempt to socialize the addict by inculcating a value system that is the opposite of that which prevailed on the street: no drugs, no deception, no stealing, and an emphasis on honesty, responsibility, and treating others as human beings rather than as objects to be exploited. Discipline in therapeutic communities is strict, penalties for breaking rules are severe, peer pressure is unrelenting, and the program assumes the role of a benevolent dictator.

Because of the strictness of the program, many residents leave against the advice, and without the permission, of the staff. The treatment group is an effective program for a limited segment of the addict population, usually those who are young, come from a middle-class background, and are highly motivated to discontinue drug abuse. Unfortunately they are very expensive programs to administer there are far fewer patients in them than in methadone maintenance programs.

EMPLOYEE ASSISTANCE PROGRAMS

BASIC EAP MODELS

The National Clearinghouse on Alcohol and Drug Abuse Information (NCADI) has designed the following outline of models for Employee Assistance Programs or EAPs. Standard EAP model programs provide tools for prevention and intervention when employees' substance abuse and other personal problems impact on job performance.

Employers may implement a single model or a hybrid model based on organizational needs and philosophy. EAPs may be managed and operated in-house, contracted to an external provider, or a combination of both.

LAY ASSESSMENT / REFERRAL MODEL

Lay Assessment or Referral Models are in-house programs staffed by recovering substance abusers. Programs where duties are assumed by human resources employees or volunteer staff also fit this category. Staff may assist in referral to self-help groups and local treatment centers. This model generally lacks education and training components and it is becoming obsolete as professional counselors and trained EAP specialists replace lay practitioners. Another option, for small employers with limited resources, is to use existing expertise in conjunction with a communicated drug policy.

PROFESSIONAL ASSESSMENT, AND REFERRAL MODEL

Under this model, professionally trained counselors are available for confidential, easy to access assistance and support. The counselor makes an initial assessment and refers troubled employees or family members to appropriate community resources.

Services may be contracted with external providers on a per employee annual basis or on an as needed, fee-for-service, case-by-case basis. Providers range from full service EAP firms to individual local physicians, social workers or psychiatric nurses with training and experience in addictions.

OUTREACH SERVICES MODEL

These are "free" or low-cost EAP services offered by hospitals and mental health and alcohol treatment facilities as a means of outreach for their various programs. Some of these services may be outstanding and small employers should consider this option.

FULL SERVICE MODEL

This is an in house program or, more likely for small employers, an externally-contracted service paid for by the employer through an annual per employee fixed fee, or basic administrative fee plus fee for service, contract.

A fixed-fee EAP is recommended so that costs are clearly defined. In addition to sessions for assessment and referral, from one to eight sessions are included in the annual fee to provide brief counseling for problems that can be resolved in short order. For many persons, short term EAP counseling will resolve the problem. Usually a 30 to 60 day program will suffice in these cases.

Substance abuse and critical psychiatric cases are referred to external treatment, as are cases requiring legal and/or financial planning consultation.

COMPREHENSIVE EAP AND GATEKEEPER MODEL

In this model, benefit plans may provide higher reimbursement of treatment costs for employees who are referred through the EAP to mental health or substance abuse treatment providers who are pre-selected (preferred provider networks). The employee is required to use the services of specific treatment centers, and is allowed increased insurance benefits for agreeing to use these services.

CONSORTIUM MODEL

This is a means for small employers to join together as an independent group through trade or other associations to increase purchasing power. The EAP providers reduce per employee costs in return for assurance of contracts with a large number of employers and a larger base of employees. The EAP may treat each employer as a separate contract, but with lower costs than if the employer obtained the services separately. The benefits are a reduction of costs based on a sliding scale, and more services at lower costs.

Under a variation of this model, sometimes called a coalition, employers band together to purchase the services of an EAP counselor who is responsible for contracting the EAP services, including negotiating and assuring account-ability.

FEE FOR SERVICE MODEL

Under this model, an employer reaches an agreement with an individual practitioner or small group to provide any of the range of EAP services on a pay-as-you-use-it basis. Such services may include on-site counseling or program promotion. This approach may assure compliance with the law with few, if any, up-front costs.

Due to the needs for confidentiality, it is difficult to monitor actual use and the employer must rely on the veracity and integrity of the provider.

INNOVATIVE MODEL FOR SMALL EMPLOYERS

Small employers may want to consider this proposal under which they would develop a list of specially trained primary care physicians (family practitioners, general practitioners). The lists would be distributed to all employees, encouraging self referrals or supervisor referrals for problems related to health and work, including substance abuse problems. Negotiations would take place but a possible agreement would be for the employer to pay a fixed fee to the physician(s), perhaps $85 to $150, on a fee-for-service basis. The physician would be paid directly by the employer in supervisor-referred cases. In self-referrals, the employee would pay the physician at each visit.

The employee would submit an invoice to his or her insurance firm for reimbursement. In the absence of medical insurance benefits, the employer could elect to arrange with the physicians to pay the costs directly.

The physician(s) would be accountable to the employer as in any basic EAP structure, including EAP use reports consistent with confidentiality requirements.

The physician(s) and appropriate office staff could perform EAP services such as education and training in conjunction with a social worker, who may be affiliated with more than one medical practice. The social worker would keep abreast of community resources for appropriate treatment referral.

Potential Benefits to Consider:

For small employers, such an idea is very attractive because there are no up front costs. Part of the pay as you go costs may be reimbursed through existing health insurance benefits, further reducing costs. Agreements with physicians can specify referral alternatives so they are consistent with health insurance coverage.

For employees, such a service is non-threatening, and may be more widely used by individuals or supervisors since any work related problem is being addressed as a medical problem.

Potential shortcomings;

There is no on sight counseling under such a program, no counseling of management on policies and programs, and no communications program for supervisors and employees developed by EAP professionals.

Self-referral may be limited because only employees who can afford to pay physicians up-front may seek services, with others not being able to wait for insurance reimbursement.

ALCOHOLICS ANONYMOUS AND "12 STEP PROGRAMS"

Alcoholics Anonymous (AA) is perhaps the best known and most successful alcoholism recovery program. The program, with its "12 steps to recovery" has also been used effectively in treating drug and other addictions.

AA was founded in the United States in 1935 by Dr. Robert Smith and Bill Wilson. By the 1990's the organization has grown to more than 93,000 groups in 131 countries, with an estimated membership of over 2 million. AA functions as a fellowship organization whose members pay no dues and may attend meetings as often as they wish. It defines alcoholism and drug abuse as a disease as well as a spiritual problem. The AA philosophy and program for recovery are stated in the 12 Steps to Recovery.

The alcoholic must recognize his or her "powerlessness over alcohol or drugs" and seek help from a "higher power" in regaining control of his or her life. Although alcoholism and addiction, according to the AA philosophy, can never be cured that is, the alcoholic can never safely drink or use drugs again, the individual can "recover" to lead a productive and normal life as long as he or she remains sober.

Since its inception the organization has also reduced popular misconceptions of alcoholics by educating both professionals and the public about the nature of alcoholism. The related organizations of Alanon and Alateen provide similar support to the families and children of alcoholics.

Other organizations, such as Overeaters Anonymous, Narcotics Anonymous, Gamblers Anonymous, and Co-Dependents Anonymous have adopted the "12-Step" program for recovery.

It is important to note that a common denominator among recovering alcoholics and drug addicts, using a 12 step program, is that of "hitting bottom". This is an experience in which the individual has given up all hope of controlling his addictive behavior through willpower or his own personal efforts.

There has been very little success with any program that attempts to coerce an individual to change his habits until or unless he has become motivated to do so.

Despite these herculean efforts and costs, the country still has a vast drug problem. The reason is simple, drug use is inevitable in a certain percentage of citizens. If this were not the case, we would have found a solution to drug use long ago.

We have allocated 41 government agencies, hundreds of billions of dollars, and seventy five years of effort, toward attempts at eradicating drugs and drug use in this country.

Is it possible that the time has come for us to consider some alternatives?

Chapter

Four

IT IS TIME FOR A NEW
GENERATION OF LEADERSHIP
TO COPE WITH NEW PROBLEMS
AND NEW OPPORTUNITIES FOR
THERE IS A NEW WORLD TO BE
WON

John F. Keneddy
July 4, 1960

DRUG USE
IN AMERICA

HOW MANY OF US USE DRUGS? WHAT TYPE? HOW OFTEN?

How prevalent is drug use in America? Well, there is good news and there is bad news. The bad news is that a huge percentage of Americans have used illegal drugs, perhaps over one third of the population. The good news, however is that a very small percentage of these users can be considered addicts, or even abusers.

It seems that the stereotypical image of a drug user, fostered by media, politicians, and self serving "community activists", have been misleading us. The average illicit drug user can not be the scruffy, bearded, dirty, minority trying to sell drugs to kids at the local school or robbing some poor innocent to pay for his habit. If this were an accurate description of an average drug user we would be overrun by 75 million of these individuals in our country.

The reality is that the average drug user is indistinguishable from you or me. He (or she) probably has a job, a family, perhaps a home, and a car. This individual uses drugs occasionally, for short periods, and then goes back to life as usual. The net effect is quite similar to someone going out for a night on the town and, perhaps, abusing alcohol.

Let's look at some facts.

Current prevalence rates for use of any illicit drug among persons 12 years of age and older decreased from 23 million drug users (12.1%) in 1985, to 14.5 million users (7.3%) in 1988 to 13 million users (6.4%) today.

The number of cocaine users decreased significantly from 2.9 million (1.5%) in 1988 to 1.6 million (0.8%) today, continuing a previous decline. This represents a decrease in the number of cocaine users since 1985, when there were an estimated 5.8 million (2.9%) cocaine users. The reduction in cocaine use may be attributable to, and offset by, the recent availability and alternate usage of crack cocaine.

Cigarette use dropped from 32% 1985 to 29% in 1988, and presently stands at 27%, representing a significant decrease from 1988. This represents a 3.5 million decrease in the number of cigarette smokers in the last two years. The previous three year period, 1985-88, experienced a 3.2 million decrease, for a total decrease of 6.7 million persons since 1985.

There are presently 102.9 million drinkers of alcoholic beverages compared with 105.8 million in 1988, and 113.1 million in 1985. The alcohol use rates in 1985, 1988, and present, for those aged 12 and over, are 59%, 53%, and 51%, respectively.

CURRENT ANALYSIS

Overall, 74.4 million Americans age 12 or older (37 percent of the population) have tried marijuana, cocaine or other illicit drugs at least once in their lifetime.

Almost 27 million Americans (13.3%) used marijuana, cocaine or other illicit drugs at least once in the past year. Among youth (12 to 17 years old), 15.9 % used an illicit drug in the past year and 8.1% used an illicit drug at least once in the past month. Comparable rates for young adults (18-25 years old) are 28.7% past year and 14.9% past month. Adults 26 years old and over the rates are 10.0% used drugs in the past year and 4.6%, in the past month.

The overall percentage of persons using illicit drugs in the past month was 6.4%. Rates for males and females are 7.9% and 5.1%, respectively.

In addition to males, other demographic subgroups with rates in excess of the overall rate are those for blacks (8.6%), large metro areas (7.3%), those living in the West region (7.3%), and the unemployed population (14.0%). Over 4.8 million or 8 percent of the 60.1 million women 15-44 years of age have used an illicit drug in the past month. Slightly over one-half million or 0.9% used cocaine and 3.9 million (6.5%) used marijuana in the past month. Among 18-34 year old full-time employed Americans, 24.4% used an illicit drug in the past year, and 10.5% used an illicit drug in the past month. Of these full-time workers, 9.2 percent used marijuana, and 2.1% used cocaine in the past month.

ANALYSIS BY DRUG

Cocaine

Among the 6.2 million people who used cocaine in the past year, 662,000 (10.6%) used the drug once a week or more and 336,000 (5.4%) used the drug daily or almost daily throughout the year. While the number of past year and past month cocaine users has decreased significantly since the peak year 1985, frequent or more intense use has not decreased. Of the 12.2 million past year cocaine users in 1985, an estimated 647,000 used the drug weekly and 246,000 used it daily or almost daily.

Rates for use of cocaine in the past year declined for youth
(12 - 17 years old) from 4% in 1985 to 2.9% in 1988 to 2.2 % presently. For young adults (aged 18-25), the rates for 1985, 1988, and current, are 16.3%, 12.1% and 7.5%, respectively. These decreases between were statistically significant for both age groups.

The rate of cocaine use in the last 30 days was 0.8% overall, a significant decrease from the 1988 rate of 1.5%. The rate of current cocaine use for males (1.1%) was over twice as high as that for females (0.5%). Other demographic subgroups for which the rates of current cocaine use are the highest were the unemployed (2.7%), blacks (1.7%), and Hispanics (1.9%).

Approximately 1.45% of the population 12 years old and over have used crack at some time in their lives, and one-half of one percent used crack during the past year. These rates changed very little from those in 1988. This translates to about one million past year crack users for per year. Past year use is highest among males (0.8%), blacks (1.7%) and the unemployed (1.3%). By age group, the highest rate is for young adults 18-25 years old (1.4%).

Marijuana

Marijuana remains the most commonly used illicit drug in the United States. Approximately 66.5 million Americans (33.1%) have tried marijuana at least once in their lives. Nearly three million youth, over 15 million young adults, and in excess of 48 million adults aged 26 and older have tried marijuana. The lifetime rate for marijuana use among youth was 14.8% while the rate for young adults was 52.2%. These rates have been steadily decreasing since 1979, when they were 31% and 68%, respectively.

The number of people currently using marijuana did not change significantly in this study, decreasing slightly from 5.9% to 5.1%. Rates were highest for males (6.4%), blacks (6.7%), and the unemployed (12.3%). Of the 20.5 million people who used marijuana (at least once) in the past year, over one-quarter, or 5.5 million, used the drug once a week or more.

Alcohol and Tobacco Products

The decline in the rates of lifetime alcohol use seen between 1985 and 1988 (from 56% to 50%) of youth ages 12 to 17, continued to decrease and is presently 48%. Past year use was 41%, and has experienced a steady decline since 1979. Today less than 25% of youth have had at least one drink during the past month. This is similar to 1988 survey results.

For young adults 18-25, the prevalence of alcoholic beverage use is substantially higher than for youth ages 12-17: 88% have tried alcohol, 80% have used alcohol in the past year, and 63% have used alcohol during the preceding month. Although this represents little change from 1988, drinking alcohol has steadily declined since 1985. The current rates for drinking among young adults in the past year and past month are significantly lower than those reported in 1985 (87% and 71%, respectively in 1985).

Of the 133 million people age 12 and older (66% of the population) who drank (alcohol) in the past year, nearly one-third, or 42 million, drank at least once a week.

Nearly three-quarters of the American population (73.2%) have tried cigarettes, and slightly over a quarter (26.7%) are past month (current) smokers - a decrease from 28.8 percent in 1988. Current use of cigarettes among youth is almost 12%; 32% among young adults; and 28% among adults 26 and over. 4% of youth and 6% of young adults used smokeless tobacco during the past month. These data indicate little change from 1988.

Of the 7.1 million current users of smokeless tobacco, over 91% are males. In contrast with patterns of illicit drug use, rates of use of smokeless tobacco are highest for whites, those living in non-metropolitan areas, and those living in the South.

Other Drugs

Hallucinogens, which first gained prominence during the mid-sixties, include such drugs as

LSD, PCP, mescaline, and peyote. Past year prevalence rates for hallucinogens decreased significantly between 1988 and today (1.6% vs.1.1%). Males (1.7%) exhibit the highest prevalence rates. Although past year usage is highest among the two age groups, 12-17 (2.4%) and 18-25 (3.9%), lifetime usage is highest among the 26-34 year old population (15.7%).

While many youth (7.8%) and young adults (10.4%) have experimented with inhalants, past month use is only 2.2% for youth and 1.2% for young adults. There were no significant changes in inhalant prevalence between 1988 and 1993.

Past month nonmedical use of psychotherapeutic drugs, i.e., sedatives, tranquilizers, stimulants, and analgesics, have stabilized at the 1988 rate of under 2% from the higher (3.2%) rate in 1985. A significant decrease was noted for past year use for the age group 18-25 and 26-34. In 1988 the rates were 11% and 10%, respectively. For 1993 they decreased to 7% and less than 6%.

This dramatic reduction translates to nearly 3 million less past year users in these two age groups.

This should not be misconstrued to mean that we are winning the war on drugs.

The fact that we see some reduction in usage, while encouraging , is insignificant to overall usage

WASHINGTON, D.C. SURVEY

91

This survey included an over sampling in the Washington, D.C. metropolitan area. Comparisons have been made between rates of drug use in the Washington, D.C. metropolitan area and the rates for all other large metropolitan areas combined. In the Washington, D.C. metropolitan area, rates for lifetime use of any illicit drug (36.5%), marijuana (33.6%) and cocaine (12.9%) were similar to rates estimated for other large metropolitan areas.

A higher rate of lifetime use of PCP (4.7% vs. 3.4%) was found in the Washington, D.C. metropolitan area when compared with all other large metropolitan areas. In low income urban areas of the Washington metropolitan area, the rate was even higher (5.9%). Although statistically not significant, the rate of lifetime use of "crack" was higher in the Washington area than in other large metropolitan areas (2.9% vs. 1.9%).

In low income urban areas of the Washington metropolitan area, the lifetime rate of "crack" use was 4.0 percent.

So What Does All This Mean?

Now that we've had a look at some of the trends and statistics regarding drug use, you may be wondering if the trend towards lower usage is a sign that we are winning the war on drugs. Unfortunately this is not the case. Overall drug usage, when evaluated on the amount consumed by the American public is up significantly.

Despite a slight trend toward a decrease in the percentage of population using drugs, an increase in population has kept the actual

number of drug users fairly consistent. The point is that we are not winning the war on drugs and we never will.

The next chapter discusses why this is the case.

Chapter

Five

The soft-minded man always fears change. He feels security in the status quo, and has an almost morbid fear of the new.
For him, the greatest pain is the pain of a new idea

Martin Luther King Jr.

THE WINDS OF CHANGE

Who, in their right mind, would suggest that we pass a law to allow the purchase of illegal drugs?

Hippies or "potheads" wanting to use marijuana without being harassed? Discouraged prosecutors tired of putting drug felons in prison, while violent criminals are being released? Disillusioned customs officers and DEA agents, who know the drug war can never be won? Civil libertarians, who want the government out of our business? Taxpayers weary of footing the bill for the war on drugs?

Perhaps all of the above, but a growing number of people and organizations in the mainstream of American society are coming to the conclusion that a major change in our drug policy could be both necessary and beneficial. The vast array of suggestions, requirements, laws, and expenses, described in Chapter Three, indicate that drug use is definitely a major problem in the U.S. This is not a major revelation. So what are we going to do about it?

Let's review the views of some of the more noteworthy Americans that have expressed the idea that there may be a better way.

William F. Buckley - Eminent conservative spokesman and author, has often questioned the wisdom of outlawing drugs due to the expense and waste inherent in trying to enforce these laws.

Jocelyn Elders - Attorney General of The United States Recently took a controversial stand in saying that drug legalization would reduce the crime rate. While her presentation of facts and knowledge of the subject seemed limited, her basic premise was sound, as the following chapters will reveal.

Milton Friedman - Professor of economics, and Nobel Prize winner, has been quoted as saying "Alcohol and tobacco cause many more deaths (650,000 per year) in users than do drugs. Decriminalization would not prevent us from treating addicts as we now treat alcoholics. We could still prohibit advertisement, and outlaw sales to minors. Moreover, if even a small fraction of the money we now spend on trying to enforce drug prohibition was devoted to treatment and rehabilitation, in an atmosphere of compassion, not punishment, the reduction in drug usage and in the harm done to users would be dramatic".

George Will - Conservative columnist, stated on **This Week with David Brinkley** that "at the very least this (drug legalization) is a subject that should be openly debated".

Sam Donaldson - Media personality, has stated the he believes "drug legalization would both reduce crime and reduce demand".

Gustapho De Greiff - Chief of the Ministry of Justice in Columbia South America, in a recent **60 MINUTES INTERVIEW** was quoted to say, "Unless something can be done to reduce the demand in the U.S. then we may as well legalize drugs, we simply cannot win this war."

Ethan Nadelmann in The Drug Legalization Debate "The past 20 years have demonstrated that a drug policy shaped by exaggerated rhetoric, designed to arouse fear, has only exacerbated our current disaster. Unless we are willing to evaluate our options logically, **including various legalization strategies**, we will run an even greater risk than we now face: We may never find the best solution to our drug problems".

George Bennett - NYPD advisor - "Drug sales should be permitted by government-licensed vendors. All drugs should be sold generically, with no brand name competition permitted".

The American Civil Liberties Union (ACLU) has consistently challenged the constitutionality of all drug laws. They are particularly interested in any act which violates search and seizure, privacy, and random testing rights.

The CATO institute and Rand Corporation "Think Tanks" are employing various scholars and experts to study drug policy and share findings.

The International Anti-prohibition League on Drugs held a conference in 1989. Representatives from 12 Western nations attended. A spokes person for the league stated "Crime resulting from outlawing drugs endangers ordinary citizens and threatens the stability of states. This modern version of prohibition has turned great cities into battlefields."

John Stuart Mill in his essay **On Liberty** once wrote "The only purpose for which power can be rightfully exercised over any member of a civilized community, against his will, is to prevent harm to others. **His own good is not a sufficient warrant.**"

We are slowly undermining our constitutional rights in order to modify the actions of some individuals. Many believe that the trade off is simply not worth it. This is compounded by the fact that we are spending billions of dollars on the drug war and making no headway in reducing drug use.

Shortage of revenue sources, coupled with the frustration and waste associated with enforcement of drug laws, have combined to form a groundswell of public opinion. **Drug reform may be an issue whose time has come.**

THE FOURTH AMENDMENT TO THE CONSTITUTION

The right of the people to be secure in their persons, houses, papers, and effects against unreasonable searches and seizures shall not be violated, and no warrants shall issue, but on probable cause, supported by oath or affirmation, and particularly describing the place to be searched, and persons or things to be seized.

The following activities have been sanctioned by our courts in recent years, in order to control drug trafficking. Do these sound like activities that our founding fathers would encourage?:

Land seizure of up to 5,000 acres is allowed if one marijuana plant is found.

Confiscation of vehicles or vessels without due process has been allowed.

Search of private property without a warrant, is allowed even if posted "No Trespassing".

Search of bank records, phone records, even trash, has been deemed to be an acceptable activity.

Roadblocks may be set up by law enforcement agencies. They now have the right to search all vehicles, trunks, glove compartments, suitcases, briefcases, etc. **All without any warrant, probable cause, or description.**

Mandatory Drug Testing has been encroaching on many work places.

Our founding fathers fought and died to revolt against such distasteful tactics.

These methods sound more like those employed by the former Soviet Union KGB or Eastern Block Communist countries than tactics employed by what is supposed to be the shining example of freedom throughout the world.

Reflect for a moment on what the last 75 years, and various stages of attempted enforcement of our drug laws has accomplished.

Have we eliminated drug use? Hardly.

As little as thirty years ago we were a different nation. Our crime rate was minimal. We left our doors unlocked. The only gang activity the country had seen was in "West Side Story". Repeat offenders were nonexistent because we had no prison overcrowding. Criminals were usually caught and were put away once and for all. Respect for law enforcement was the norm.

What happened?

Drugs Happened! Our attempts to escalate and enforce the war on drugs has not only cost us billions, but in the meantime drugs have financed a rampant increase in crime. Drugs and our ineffective enforcement efforts have sabotaged the respect that criminals used to have for law enforcement.

What else could we have done with the hundreds of billions of dollars that we have spent on the war on drugs?

We must make a choice between our desire to stop the proliferation of drug use in this country (a nice dream which we can NEVER accomplish) and our willingness to give up our individual freedoms as guaranteed by the Constitution.

OUR POWER TO CHOOSE

The single most powerful tool possessed by every person on this planet is **OUR POWER TO CHOOSE**. We often forget that we have this power, some of us go through life and never even realize we have it.

Every day of our lives we make literally thousands of decisions. Even the decision to do nothing is a decision. Whether we like it or not we are where we are in this world as a direct result of the decisions we have made. It's not the fault of anyone else if we are not happy with our current situation. The blame, or accolades are exactly where they belong, squarely on our shoulders.

If we are unhappy with our current situation, who made the ultimate decisions that put us in this situation? **WE DID.** If we are unhappy or irritated, who decided how we were going to react? **WE DID!**

This is a worrisome revelation to many people, they don't want to hear it. The last thing they want to think is that all their excuses for all their failures are lies they've been telling themselves.

Not hearing it, or not thinking about it does not make the reality of the fact go away, however. We can kid ourselves until the day we die, we will only hurt ourselves.

Once we have come to terms with the fact that we are completely responsible for every aspect of our lives, some very wonderful things can begin to happen. For one thing this realization gives us the freedom to act as we see fit in ANY situation. If we're at a party, for example, and we decide that we are not enjoying ourselves, we can leave. But this philosophy goes much beyond our individual ability to make personal choices. If we agree that we are completely responsible for our own decisions **SO IS EVERYONE ELSE.**

From this moment on, you have the power to decide every single aspect of your life. Actually you always had this power, but you may not have known it. The wonderful freedom in knowing that you no longer have to react with anger at the behavior of someone else is very enlightening. If you decide to smile the next time someone cuts you off on the freeway, you will find it a truly unique experience.

Another aspect of this concept is the fact that you are no longer responsible for, and in fact have no control whatever over, the reactions or feelings of someone else. That is where **THEIR POWER TO CHOOSE** comes in.

What does all this have to do with **THE DRUG SOLUTION?** Everything. If we agree that we are all ultimately responsible for our own feelings and actions, and that we have little if any responsibility, or for that matter control over the feelings or actions of another. What right do we have to tell that person how to lead his life? We have no right whatever to exercise any control over another until or unless that person harms the person or property of another.

If the person chooses to harm himself, with drugs for example, it is none of our business, until he harms the person or property of some other individual. That is what we need laws to accomplish, and that is what the fourth amendment to the constitution was designed to insure.

If someone decides he wants to take drugs and we decide to try to stop him we have broken our law of ultimate responsibility. If he decides to abuse drugs, forces will come into play that dwarf the powers of us puny humans. The law of ultimate responsibility will eventually make a drug abuser miserable, because he is not doing that which he was put here to do. This law never fails.

If we as a society try to impose our moral wishes on another, we are trying to take away his power to choose. This is what we try to do when we put someone in prison. There are many good reasons to incarcerate someone, but **all of them include harming the person or property of another.** Putting someone in prison for something he chooses to do to himself robs him of the lesson he would have learned if left to his own devices.

Infinitely worse is what happens to a society that tries to impose these "laws of morality". We, as a society are suffering from many of the effects of our attempts to make people behave as we think they should. Virtually every major social ill that currently plagues our society can be traced to our well intentioned but misguided attempts to legislate morality. The recent collapse of the U.S.S.R. should be a dire warning of the ultimate failure of repressive societies.

Many people feel that we cannot win this war on drugs without becoming a repressive "Big Brother" type of society. Some are beginning to ask, "Is it possible that we can turn this problem into an advantage"?

How could we begin to benefit from the billions of dollars that we now waste on incarceration, enforcement, and prosecution of drug dealers? How could we benefit from the sales of all these drugs? The following chapters discuss these question and offer some very viable alternatives to our existing policies.

Chapter

Six

YE SHALL KNOW THE
TRUTH AND THE TRUTH
SHALL MAKE YOU MAD!

Aldous Huxley

THE PROBLEM

Drug use in America, is the single biggest problem facing our country today. It's not the deficit. It's not organized crime, or gang violence. It's not prison overcrowding. It's not government overspending. It's not foreign competitors. It's not unemployment. **IT'S DRUG USE, DRUG SALES, AND DRUG ENFORCEMENT PLAIN AND SIMPLE.**

How can this "back shelf" problem be defined as our primary dilemma? Simply because illicit drug use, directly and indirectly, is the primary cause of, **and the potential solution too**, all the above named problems. **Logically addressing this problem has the potential to solve most or all of our other social ills.**

Let's take some examples:

GANGS AND ORGANIZED CRIME

Most of the income of gangs and organized crime is derived from illegal activity, primarily illegal drug sales. We can have no reduction in these groups or their power until we reduce or eliminate the incredible income these criminals generate through this illegal activity. If we can eliminate this primary source of income for these groups while, at the same time, offer legitimate employment opportunities as an alternative, the problem becomes self-correcting.

PRISON AND COURT OVERCROWDING

58% of the detainees in our prisons and jails are incarcerated solely due to nonviolent drug related offenses relating to use, sale, or production of illicit drugs. Between 1981 and 1988, the height of the drug war, prison populations increased by over 90%, the vast majority being drug offenders. **No appreciable reduction in drug use was realized during this period.**

Let's look at some additional facts. According to the National Clearinghouse for Alcohol and Drug Information (NCADI):

33.2% OR 67 MILLION AMERICANS uses or has used marijuana or hashish.

11.5% OR 23 MILLION AMERICANS uses or has used cocaine.

1.3% OR 2.6 MILLION AMERICANS uses or has used heroin.

25% of the American public uses illegal drugs at least once a year.

AN INCREDIBLE 33% OF THE AMERICAN PUBLIC HAS USED AN ILLEGAL DRUG AT LEAST ONCE. In any group of three people, the chances are that one is, or has been, a drug user. **We can never put one third of America in jail, and if we could, we wouldn't want to.**

This represents the percentage of Americans that **admitted drug use.** It is quite likely that the true percentage is somewhat higher. Perhaps a great deal higher.

We must ask ourselves; "Just how effective do we want our enforcement people to be?" If law enforcement was 100% effective in enforcing all drug laws, we would have **67 million people in jail at a cost of over $2 TRILLION per year.**

The president of the United States, **Bill Clinton**, by his own admission, should have been convicted of a felony. Although he claims that he never inhaled the marijuana he experimented with, the mere act of holding and puffing on a joint put him at risk of a felony conviction. This example is repeated millions of times throughout the country. What would otherwise be considered all- American citizens are using drugs, on a recreational basis, with little or no lasting negative impact. They are then put in a position of risking career-threatening convictions in order to pursue their entertainment of choice. We may not agree with their decisions, but we are powerless to stop them. Let's examine some facts about the true "average drug user".

The average U.S. citizen has a stereotypical view of the average drug user as a homeless, AIDS infected, bum that just robbed someone to pay for his fix. While this type of individual certainly exists, the average drug user in no way fits this profile. Let's look at some facts revealed by surveys conducted by The Department of Labor Substance Abuse Information Database (SAID).

DRUG USE AMONG WORKING ADULTS

There is little doubt that illicit drugs are used by working adults in this country. Although employed people may have lower drug use rates than the unemployed, (Kandel, 1980) employment does not eradicate the urge to use drugs.

It is also worth noting that drug use among high school students, as reflected in the National Survey of High School Students (Johnston, O'-Malley & Bachman, 1987), is probably not dramatically different from the young adult working population. It is unlikely that most youths cease their drug use upon entering the work place. These assumptions are supported by empirical evidence gathered primarily from two sources: (1) self-report surveys, and (2) the results from an increasing number of drug testing programs in industry. Furthermore, an examination of the caseload characteristics of Employee Assistance Programs (EAPs) reveals significant percentages of employees seeking help for drug use and abuse problems. These programs, as discussed earlier, are quite effective, **if the individual wants help.**

Most of what is known about drug use in the work place comes from studies that are severely limited by their sampling (confined to a region, industry or age group) and the variables measured (often merely the results of a drug test). Consequently, very little is known about patterns, dynamics and circumstances of drug use in the work place. Moreover, the self report survey and chemical testing carry their own set of strengths and weaknesses as methods for estimating drug use prevalence. This survey was intended to: (1) present national prevalence data on drug use among working adults, and (2) examine the central methods for estimating the extent of drug use in the work place.

SURVEY OF WORKING ADULTS

In 1985, the Gallup Organization questioned 3,000 adults age 18 and older about their use of marijuana and cocaine on confidential, self-administered answer sheets. The survey was conducted on behalf of the Social Research Group of George Washington University in conjunction with a grant from the National Institute on Drug Abuse.

The survey consisted of face to face interviews with members of households throughout the United States. Of those interviewed, 1,716 adults were employed in jobs outside the home; the balance were students, housewives, or retirees. This analysis examined the drug use of the sample of employed adults and attempted to identify the groups of employed adults most in need of drug prevention, education, and treatment programs.

Two measures of drug use, current use and past-year use, are used in the analysis. Interviewees were asked, "When was the most recent time you took (the drug)?" Current users are defined as those who said they used marijuana or cocaine within the past 30 days. Recent users are adults who reported use in the past year.

To describe patterns of drug use among employed adults and identify specific groups of employees with higher rates of drug use prevalence, estimates of marijuana and cocaine use were calculated by: 1) occupational category and 2) selected socio-demographic characteristics of the employees.

RESULTS

Drug Use by Job Category

Overall, 18 percent of the total sample reported recent use of marijuana, and 6 percent reported recent use of cocaine. The sample reported current marijuana and cocaine use of 11 percent and 2 percent, respectively.

Significant differences were found among occupational categories in current marijuana use; no differences were found in current cocaine use. Current marijuana use rates ranged from 7 percent for professional managerial and clerical personnel to 16 percent for the skilled trades. Current cocaine use ranged from 1 percent to 5 percent among laborers. Past year use rates of the two substances were considerably higher, ranging from 13 percent to 22 percent for marijuana and 2 percent to 11 percent for cocaine, but the differences were not statistically significant.

The vast majority of drug users are not addicts, any more than all drinkers are alcoholics. The average drug user is the average American citizen, the addict is the exception to the rule, the addict is the person who took his habit too far and could not control himself.

This is one reason why our drug policy is self defeating. We are trying to enforce laws that Mr. and Mrs. America are breaking. The result is a devastating loss of respect for law enforcement in general, and billions of dollars in costs.

WHY OUR DRUG LAWS CAN NEVER WORK

Let's explore our current situation. We currently have 41 federal and state government agencies combating the sale and use of illegal drugs. Following are some examples of the lunacy behind our current attempts at controlling drug sales.

We begin by expending a tremendous amount of the time, money, and resources available to our local police officials, and our federal agencies, to track down and capture a drug pusher. Next we spend money (about $100 a day) to incarcerate him while awaiting trial. In many cases our next step is to provide a public defender for the pusher because he claims he has no money to pay for his own attorney thus incurring further costs. He is then sent through the court system. Often he is released back to the streets and is selling drugs again in a short time due to plea bargaining or improper arrest methods.

A common complaint of police officers is that the dealer is back on the street before the officer can complete the arrest paperwork.

If the district attorney can actually navigate the rules and laws designed to protect the innocent, and subsequently get a criminal conviction, this individual will receive an incredibly short sentence due to the lack of prison space. He will also have his sentence reduced 25 to 50% automatically for "good behavior". Good behavior in today's prison system is granted to practically anyone who doesn't kill a prison guard. While this individual languishes in prison with his court ordered comforts like color TV, weight training, great food, and free education, **he is spending an additional $30,000 a year of our money!** This is the average annual cost of housing a prisoner in the United States.

There are currently about 300,000 prisoners in city, state, and federal facilities on non-violent drug offense convictions.

To add insult to injury, the very minute this criminal was removed from the street, another was in line to begin selling the illicit drugs in his place.

Another negative impact of enforcing our drug laws is that of turning an individual that had previously been an economic asset to society into an economic liability. While we may detest an the fact that an average citizen would use drugs as a form of entertainment, catching and convicting him is tantamount to shooting ourselves in the foot.

Assume that the average drug user is a working, tax paying citizen. One day law enforcement catches him in the act of using drugs. Not only does this individual's life alter drastically, but we now have to support him. He has entered a downward spiral that will quite often wind up in converting this person to a life of crime. If he is convicted of a felony, he will likely serve prison time, lose his job, and be unable to get a job when he is released. He will be bitter at a society that ruined his life with a ridiculous and unfair law. The only training he will get in prison will teach him how to pursue a criminal lifestyle. When you multiply this story by 300,000 people you begin to realize why we have a crime problem. This scenario is much more likely to occur in our inner cities resulting in a attitude of hoplessness that fosters more drug use, and more criminal activity.

The sale of drugs is so well coordinated in America that even huge drug busts have practically no effect on distribution. The drug lords consider this loss of product and personnel as a cost of doing business and on our very best days we don't intercept over 10% of the drugs coming into this country.

More than half of all illicit drugs currently sold in the world are sold in the United States.

We are extremely ineffective at actually imprisoning the top management of the drug distribution organizations. When we do "catch a big fish", we spend another small fortune trying to convict him. The drug king pin, of course, has virtually unlimited resources to spend for his defense. He got it from selling the drugs. In the rare case where we incarcerate one of these individuals, he either continues to run his operation from prison, or turns it over to one of his "generals".

A secondary effect of the inevitable prison overcrowding caused by enforcing our current drug laws, is that convicted murderers, rapists, and other hardened criminals, are released onto our streets every day because we cannot afford to build new prisons to house them. This leads to what is currently referred to as "the revolving door policy". When we arrest, convict, and sentence a drug pusher and he enters prison, another, possibly much worse, individual is simultaneously being released.

ACCORDING TO A RECENT SURVEY, CONVICTED MURDERERS SERVE <u>AN AVERAGE OF 3.8 YEARS IN PRISON</u> FOR THEIR CRIME. It is easy to understand why our crime problem has escalated in an unprecedented way in recent years. Prison sentences no longer intimidate felons.

Let's assume that a hired killer, a mafia "hit man" for example was to be paid $250,000 to murder someone that was trying to move in on a major drug dealer. The drug dealer hires this paid killer, who then commits this heinous crime, and is subsequently caught, convicted, and sentenced. If he then served the average sentence for murder, 3.8 years, **HE WOULD WIND UP EARNING $65,789 A YEAR FOR A MURDER CONVICTION.** What's worse, this is tax free unreported income, so we don't even collect taxes on this money. We also PAY $25-30,000 to house him in prison for the term of his sentence.

If we could provide a **SOLUTION** that would eliminate the incentive for those people who sell drugs, we would eventually free up the **58% of our prison space currently being taken up by nonviolent drug related offenders.** We would then have no problem housing those felons, like the hired killer described above, that really need to be imprisoned for long periods of time. Since people would no longer be selling drugs illegally, we would no longer have to put them in prison. We may wish people wouldn't use drugs but wishing will never make it so.

118

**We must consider how to turn this tremen-
dously negative predicament, that is draining our economy, into a positive situation
that provides positive benefits to our
citizens.**

Prior to about 1920 we had no drug laws in this
country. Many forms of opium, cocaine, and
marijuana were available upon demand. Coca
Cola, in it's original form, was formulated with
significant amounts of cocaine. Despite these
facts the number of users and abusers prior to
1920, as a percent of population, was approximately the same as it is today.

**DRUG ENFORCEMENT, LIKE PROHIBI-
TION, DOES NOT AND CANNOT WORK IN
A FREE COUNTRY.**

FREE   ENTERPRISE

Our country's entire belief system is based on
the premise that free enterprise works. The law
of supply and demand dictates that as long as
people want drugs like cocaine, marijuana,
crack, or heroin, they will get them. If we put
one pusher in jail, the incredible profit
generated by the drug business dictates that
another individual will instantly fill in the gap.

The fact is that our meager attempts to enforce
the drug laws only subsidize the drug lords. By
driving up the price of the 90% of the drugs we
are unable to intercept, we are actually improv-
ing the profits of the drug lords, street gangs,
and organized crime.

**THE ONLY REALISTIC WAY TO
ELIMINATE DRUG USE IN THIS
COUNTRY IS TO REDUCE OR DESTROY**

THE PERSONAL FREEDOMS OF EVERY CITIZEN IN THE COUNTRY.

Take the example of the **"ZERO TOLERANCE"** policy used by the Drug Enforcement Agency (DEA), and many local law enforcement organizations. This law allows the DEA to confiscate property of suspected drug dealers **BEFORE ANY COURT HEARING, WITHOUT DUE PROCESS, WITHOUT EVEN HAVING BEEN CHARGED WITH A CRIME.**

Imagine for a moment you have a teenage son. He's allowed to take the family car out for a Friday evening. A friend of his has a marijuana cigarette with him. they are subsequently caught and arrested for possession. **THIS LAW WOULD ALLOW THE PERMANENT CONFISCATION OF YOUR CAR.** God forbid that your son has any drugs of his own at home. This could cause the immediate confiscation of your home, car, furniture, and 25 inch color TV.

Sound farfetched? Ask David Phelps a shrimp fisherman from Key West. The Coast Guard confiscated his $250,000 shrimper when the butt of a single marijuana cigarette was found aboard.

While the motive behind the creation this law is understandable, it is not the kind of trend that most Americans find desireable or acceptable. Zero Tolerance is a law that was born out of frustration.

We are asking law enforcement to enforce our drug laws while, at the same time, to attempt the impossible; control the access and use of a desired product in a free country. **IT CAN'T BE DONE!** We, as a society, are probably not willing to give up our rights and freedoms in order to solve our social problems or the drug problem.

This is not to say that the DEA and law enforcement agents are bad people. They are, in fact dedicated, hard-working, individuals that put their life on the line in a vain attempt to eradicate drugs in this country. Unfortunately, they have been assigned the impossible task of eliminating a product that is in high demand in a free country.

AMERICANS ARE USED TO GETTING WHAT THEY WANT, ASSUMING THEY HAVE THE MONEY TO PAY FOR IT. WHETHER WHAT THEY WANT IS A NEW CAR, A HOME, A GUN, OR A GRAM OF COCAINE, THEY WILL GET THAT WHICH THEY DESIRE. This is not a fact that we can, or should, change.

The only way the DEA and local law enforcement agencies, can begin to slow down the importation of drugs in America is to begin usurping our individual rights whether we are breaking the law or not! Even these drastic steps have obviously been largely ineffective. Anyone, anywhere in the United States that decides he wants a gram of cocaine, a shot of heroin, or an ounce of marijuana can have it within 24 hours, and in most cases within a half hour. After billions of dollars have been spent on our useless attempt to eliminate illegal drugs in our country, we are no closer than the day we started over 75 years ago. We might as well face the facts: We are not winning the war on drugs and we never will.

We will never be successful in eliminating or significantly reducing drug use in this country. Using force or laws as a means of repression is ineffective and self defeating. Have we learned nothing from the lessons of the Soviet Union? We must come to terms with the fact that drugs are here to stay until the day that the last individual in this country **decides for himself** that the drug abuse lifestyle is no longer what he chooses. Drug use is an individual choice. It may be a bad choice, but that doesn't change the fact that the individual must decide for himself that he is not going to use drugs. Unfortunately some very unpleasant things must happen to some people before they realize what is best for them. Some never learn, they die, but we as a society cannot control this behavior. Seventy-five years of trying to eradicate drugs, with no success, has proven this beyond any doubt.

Prohibition, in the 1920's was a good example of a useless attempt at trying to control a desired substance in a free economy. It was totally ineffective. Alcohol was as available as ever during prohibition, and all that resulted was a huge waste of resources and a lot of people laughing at law enforcement officials behind their backs. Another problem with prohibition was that the illicit earnings, produced by black market liquor, financed the beginnings of organized crime in this country.

Another timely example of our eroding rights is that of firearms. Congress recently passed the **Brady Bill** in an attempt to curb the availability of guns to criminals. Does it seem fair that law abiding citizens should be inconvenienced in order to keep criminals in check?

Besides the fact that this law will do nothing to keep guns away from criminals, it is unconstitutional.

The law of supply and demand always works. Unfortunately it also works when the product demanded is guns desired by criminals. If we completely outlawed all guns today, criminals would still get guns. We would not be able to house the criminals that we caught breaking the law against gun possession, because our prisons are already overcrowded. So why bother? While Mr. Brady is an honorable, and upstanding American, the bill bearing his name is a joke, and a step in the wrong direction. This type of "feel good legislation" deludes the public that our leaders are doing something to curb violent crime. It is an insult to our intelligence to assume that the public believes that these types of laws will have any effect whatever on our crime problems.

We are currently using unrealistic, and unworkable programs that must be drastically modified for the betterment of our nation. We can no longer afford the billions of wasted dollars, the mass of humanity clogging our prison and court systems, and the demoralized attitude of our law enforcement people in trying to accomplish the impossible. Our current system incorporates the dichotomy of trying to outlaw a desired product in a free country. This is simply an impossible task. Either the product will be sold in order to fill the demand, or the country will no longer be free.

One might argue that drugs are not just typical desired products, like a VCR or a minivan. The rules, however, are exactly the same for illegal drugs as for any other product. If the public demands and will pay for a product or service, and there is enough profit to generate the motivation, someone, somewhere will provide the desired product or service. This has been true since the first cave men traded arrowheads for fish.

If you are willing to give up your personal rights against unreasonable search and seizure, freedom to travel without communist-like check points and to generally become a police state, we might possibly be able to eliminate illegal drugs in this country. A case can be made that even these drastic steps would be ineffectual, as they have not worked in many of the more repressive countries in the world.

In Iran for example, Ayatollah Khalkhalki, whose nickname was "The Butcher" was given the power to execute, without hearing or trial, anyone found with drugs. Within a two month period he killed over 250 people. When he was criticized because the drug problem was not eliminated, he was quoted as saying "If we wanted to kill everyone found with drugs we would have to kill 5,000 people, and that would be difficult". The Ayatollah has a gift for understatement.

If you, like most people in this country, are not willing to see your freedoms eroded, then read on. The only viable alternative is within these pages. As a bonus, virtually every social ill that currently befuddles our government leaders could be addressed and resolved by **THE DRUG SOLUTION.**

THE HIDDEN COSTS OF THE DRUG WAR

We are currently spending **$12 billion,** on a nationwide basis, year in and year out, in our vain attempt to enforce our drug laws.

Not only are we spending billions on trying to accomplish the impossible, but additional billions are being lost due to related negatives.

For example:

58% of the 600,000+ criminals now in prison are there solely for selling drugs or breaking drug laws. This equates to over **300,000 prisoners.**

Just the cost of housing, monitoring, and feeding these criminals in prison is about **$15.7 billion per year!**

An additional hidden cost is that, if these prisoners were converted to useful, taxpaying citizens, we would realize another **$2 billion** in income taxes, instead of spending the $15.7 billion for their incarceration.

What about the sales of consumer products and the subsequent sales taxes these 300,000 prisoners are not generating?

If we did not need to house these individuals, we would eliminate our prison over crowding, thus saving an additional **$50 billion** proposed in state and federal dollars for new prison construction.

All told, these hidden costs represent a difference of **$75 BILLION** in available cost reductions, and increased revenue.

To paraphrase senator William Proxmier, "A billion here and a billion there, pretty soon you're talking about real money".

How can our society begin to turn this liability into an asset?

OUR DRUG POLICY IS DESTROYING OUR FUTURE

Another much more sinister and subtle problem with our current drug policy is the devastating effect on a large percentage of our population. This does not refer to the drug users. The users are making choices and living with the consequences. The real problem lies in the negative impact that the drug black market has on our inner city youth, minority population, and poverty ridden. A common scenario is that a young black male, struggling in school, sees a local drug dealer in a flashy car, living an enviable lifestyle, and apparently enjoying the American dream. This young man is irresistibly drawn to the easy life he envisions by following in the drug dealers footsteps. He drops out of school. "Who needs school, I'm going to get rich selling drugs." He thinks. He may be paid $200 or $300 to deliver an ounce or two of cocaine. Before long he has been arrested, has a record or a prison sentence, and any chance he had of legitimate employment has vanished. Many states have mandatory prison sentences for anyone caught with a minimum amount of drugs in their possession. The drug king pins know this and send young "rookies" out to do the selling and delivering. This scenario is duplicated in the poor Hispanic, Asian, and to a lesser extent, white communities throughout the country. If we could remove this incentive to take the easy way out,

126

we would encourage a return to the work ethic. We would stop raising an entire generation of minorities and poor people to have no better future than to occupy the prisons that we never stop building.

How can we provide hope and a bright future to our minority and inner city populations?

THE TRUTH ABOUT OUR PRISONS

The awful truth about our current prison system is that all we are doing is breeding the criminals that we want to get rid of. Our prisons do not educate, or rehabilitate. They do not prepare anyone for anything but a return to a life of crime. When we arrest someone for drug possession or drug sales, all we accomplish is a forced criminal education. The education is not one that includes the three R's unless the three R's include Robbery, Rape, and Recidivism.

SIX THOUSAND PEOPLE ARE MURDERED EVERY YEAR BY REPEAT FELONS. Criminals that should be in prison for long sentences are back on the streets after very minimal time actually served. Our current prison overcrowding results in the early release of the criminals that really do serious harm to our society. Every one of these murder victims can be attributed, at least indirectly, to our useless attempt to make a crime out of that which is not a crime.

A felony conviction is no longer a serious matter to a criminal that has been through the prison system. He has gotten used to the "three hots and a cot". He can live with, and in some cases prefers, the predictable routine of prison life. Society would love to lock up these multiple offenders and throw away the key. Unfortunately eighty-percent of these felons will be out on the street again. After a prison sentence they are likely to be more ruthless than ever. An ex-convict is likely to be high school drop out, have no skills, and in all probability he has never even applied for a job. How are these people going to act? It is inevitable. They may try to find a job. They will probably fail, become financially destitute, commit any number of crimes, eventually get caught and return to prison.

How can we end this vicious cycle of poverty, unemployment, hopelessness and crime?

OUR ERODING VALUES

The above scenario, combined with unemployment, and a general feeling of hopelessness in our inner cities has resulted in the deterioration in the self image of a large percentage of our population. A drug dealer, an ex-convict, or an unemployed minority does not perceive of himself as a potential executive. He has learned, in prison or on the streets, that violence, and crime are the only way to win. This may stem from the subtle message of the prison guard with a gun, or the more obvious lessons learned on tough streets, rife with drug dealers and drive by shootings. Both teach that the stronger, more violent, and better armed person wins. A man that will perpetrate violence upon another has no respect for himself or the victim. Sabotaging an individual's self esteem will inevitably result in deteriorated family values. If a man does not respect himself, he has no hope of raising a strong well adjusted family. These facts are the reasons behind some very disturbing statistics:

One million two hundred thousand illegitimate children born in this country last year. The breakdown in family values is one root cause of our problems in this country. We can no longer afford the luxury of hiding our heads in the sand. The black illegitimacy rate is **68% of all births.** Over two-thirds of all black children are coming into this world without a father. How can these mothers hope to raise solid, well adjusted children in the adverse circumstances of today's inner city?

In the white community illegitimacy is at an all time high of **22%**. If we do nothing, by the end of the century the illegitimacy rates will be **80% for blacks and 40% for whites.** All indications are that we will see simultaneous increases in the crime rates, prison populations, and poverty that is in direct proportion to the increase in illegitimacy.

How do we improve the self esteem of our inner city populations, increase employment levels, and begin to rebuild our family structure?

DID DRUGS KILL POLLY KLASS?

The recent abduction, at knife point, and subsequent murder of Polly Klass of Petaluma, California whipped the nation into a frenzy. There were calls for gun control laws, even though Polly was strangled. There was a "Three Strikes and your out law" proposed to insure permanent incarceration of three time convicted felons. The nation wept for Polly and her family.

The truth of the matter is that Richard Allen Davis, Polly's alleged murderer, would have been in prison if it weren't for our war on drugs. He had an extensive rap sheet and numerous previous convictions including kidnapping. He would have been in prison **if we had the room to house him.**

One wonders if Polly would be alive today if we had never begun putting people in jail for engaging in nonviolent drug use activity.

The drastic increase in prisoners being held on drug charges has caused the early release of all prisoners. When we put one prisoner in jail for a drug offense, another is going out the back door and he may well be much worse for society.

We cannot ignore the fact that Richard Allen Davis claimed he was high on drugs when he perpetrated his heinous crime. **But the fact is that he would have still been in prison if there was no War on Drugs.**

This sad story has been repeated hundreds. perhaps thousands, of times, and may well be the underlying reason that violent crime is the number one concern of our citizens today.

How can we solve the problem of rampant violence as well as our numerous other social problems?

Next we begin to **ANSWER** the critical questions asked throughout this chapter.

Chapter

Seven

WHATEVER MUST HAPPEN

EVENTUALLY SHOULD

HAPPEN   IMMEDIATELY

Henry A. Kissinger

THE DRUG SOLUTION

How could the United States of America afford to:

INJECT OVER **$185 BILLION A YEAR** INTO OUR ECONOMY

ELIMINATE THE DEFICIT

PROVIDE A JOB FOR EVERYONE

ELIMINATE ORGANIZED CRIME AND GANGS

MAKE EVERY STREET IN THE NATION SAFE AGAIN

SOLVE OUR OVERCROWDED PRISON SITUATION

RELIEVE OUR CLOGGED COURT SYSTEM.

ALL WITHOUT RAISING A SINGLE PENNY IN YOUR TAXES

The answer is simple. The U.S. government must go into the business of selling what are now defined as illegal drugs.

At first glance this sounds like a ridiculous, irresponsible, perhaps even dangerous statement. But let's look at some facts. As discussed in the last chapter, drug use in America is inevitable and cannot be stopped by any constitutional means. Ineffective attempts at drug enforcement are draining our economy, clogging our courts and prisons, and financing gangs and organized crime. To add insult to injury, Mr. and Mrs. America are footing the bill for the enormous costs of this lost cause and they don't get any benefit whatever from the sale of these products.

On the contrary these sales currently lead to tremendous expense and heartache as a result of the related crime and death now associated with drug sales. Why not try turning the biggest negative in the country into a positive? We have, at our finger tips, an unbelievable source of revenue and we are spending billions of dollars per year trying to get rid of it. Let's do a complete 180 degree reversal and start taking advantage of the inevitable, and begin benefiting from it!

We must begin looking at the problem as an opportunity, eliminating our self righteous demand that others live their lives as we wish they would. If we get rid of our prejudiced view, and begin looking at this problem in a rational, businesslike manner, we will see the logic of taking this action. We can begin towards a new trend that will benefit our country in unbelievably positive ways. How could such a radical proposal be implemented? Should it be implemented? That's for you the American public to decide.

DRUG LEGALIZATION

Many arguments for drug legalization have been made in the past. A few of our government officials and economists such as Milton Freidman have even had the moxy to make a case for drug legalization. Many more believe in it but are unwilling to express their views due to the political dangers and the immediate attack by the press and others.

While the points made by those in favor of drug legalization are, for the most part, well thought out and valid, they simply do not go far enough. The majority of the arguments in favor of drug legalization point out that our law enforcement officers would be relieved of the task of trying to enforce this "prohibition of the 90's". This would release manpower and resources to enforce those laws that most negatively impact society. We would also reduce the tremendous pressure on the court system due to the fact that selling drugs, of itself, would no longer be illegal. Thus, there would be fewer arrests and less cases. This would further free up our overburdened prison systems by granting amnesty or parole to those who have been convicted solely of drug sales. These are all reasonable arguments but they have a number of flaws.

For one thing, the end result of simple legalization would be that we would still have the same bad element selling the drugs, the same drug-related murders, gang and turf wars. We would still have the drug related crime from the drug users, desperate for drugs, committing robberies, car thefts, muggings, and other crimes. The current vicious cycle of drug arrests, imprisonment, release, and arrest again would not be broken. The problem of rampant violent crime would not be solved. We would not eliminate organized crime, or drug cartels and the subsequent massive expenditures we now waste in order to try to control these criminals.

THE DRUG SOLUTION offers a sensible, workable alternative to our current expensive, ineffective methods of trying to control illicit drug sales. We must completely remove the incentives for drug users to buy drugs from their current sources. **We do this by removing the profit of the sales from organized crime, gangs, and drug cartels and converting these profits into TAXES that can thereby be used to BENEFIT our country and solve our social problems.**

Aren't we as a society a bit weary of paying good taxes to support the incarceration of drug criminals who then spend our money watching TV, playing pool, and then selling their stories for a TV miniseries? Let's give them a taste of what it's like to work for a living, pay taxes, and see some of those taxes go towards housing criminals. Let's take away his previous source of illegal income, get him off his backside and make him WORK for a living!

The end result would be that all drugs that are now illegal would be purchased, distributed, and sold through a government agency The resulting profits would be used to the betterment of our country. The drugs will be sold for the same price as they command in today's black market. In fact, we already have the manpower, offices, and knowledge in place to begin. Under this proposal The Drug Enforcement Administration (DEA) would have its objectives and job description, drastically redefined. They would be required and budgeted to ACQUIRE drugs in those countries, and from those sources that currently provide the drugs.

This would of course require a complete reversal of assignments and duties of the agents. After working for so long to eradicate drugs, being assigned the task of acquiring them for distribution would be quite an adjustment for many. It should be considered, however, that many DEA agents have long been frustrated with the lack of success of our current strategies. A new tact might well prove refreshing to a good number of these motivated and intelligent public servants.

The thought of having virtually unlimited funds for drug rehabilitation programs, and interdiction of any drug lord holdouts may be very attractive. Further, the thought of a new direction for the DEA with a realistic, and achievable goal of destroying organized crime, drug cartels, and street gangs in a very short period of time, might be tremendously motivating to these agents. Perhaps a doubling of the salary of these agents would further soften the blow of redefining their objectives. In any case, filling any positions opened by agents not wishing to participate in the new program will not be a difficult task.

A side benefit could be realized by setting up networks that involve the governments of the countries providing the drugs so that they too could benefit from these sales. We thereby legitimize the farmers that grow these crops and make them taxpayers in their own country. Mexico, Columbia, Bolivia, and Peru for example are all major suppliers of drugs to the U.S. These countries are all in need of a new income source. All they would need to do would be to offer the farmers and processors a legitimate alternative to their current method of distribution. Bolivia, the poorest country in

South America, has 400,000 farmers dependent on the production of cocaine and marijuana.

According to Stephen Green acting head of the Drug Enforcement Administration the DEA agents already know who, where, and how to arrange the purchases at the current rates in those countries. The agents would simply form a working agreement with the Columbian government, for example, and make purchases directly and exclusively through the governments or their authorized agents, then arrange shipments back to the U.S. The fact that this would no longer be illegal activity, for authorized farmers, distributors, government agencies, and personnel, would provide a further reduction in costs and subsequently more profit to our government and the governments of the respective foreign countries.

We can safely assume that the foreign countries which currently have laws against drug trafficking would quickly modify those laws and follow the lead of the U.S. The foreign governments will jump at the chance to provide highly saleable products to such a major user thereby reaping the rewards of subsequent sales. The diversity and number of countries involved will insure a competitive atmosphere thereby insuring availability of the drugs at the current price with no significant increase in acquisition costs.

Once the purchase is made, and the drugs are transported to the U.S. **the value increases by about 6000%**. A Kilo (2.3 pounds) of cocaine, for example, sells in Columbia for about $1,500. If we began buying through the Columbian or Peruvian governments for say $2,500, it would provide a much needed revenue source to these underdeveloped countries. The $1,000 increase in the price paid would provide a tremendous resource to the foreign governments. We would also be provide legitimate income to the farmers and refiners currently supplying the drugs in those foreign countries.

The incredible fact is that the same kilo of cocaine that can be purchased in South America for $1,500 sells in the U.S. for about $90,000. In California, a recent cocaine confiscation of "one-half ton of cocaine" was valued at $45 million according to the DEA. **That's about $87,500 profit per kilo. A kilo is 2.2 pounds. The DEA estimates that about 125 TONS OF PURE COCAINE WAS SHIPPED INTO THE UNITED STATES LAST YEAR.** The cocaine sold on the street has been cut to about 25% strength. In other words the country is now buying about **500 TONS OF COCAINE PER YEAR. THAt'S 1,000,000 POUNDS OF CUT COCAINE, 16,000,000 OUNCES**.

(125 tons = 250,000 pounds. Each pound becomes 4 pounds after being cut. 4 X 250,000 pounds = 1 million pounds of cut cocaine. There are 16 ounces in a pound 16 X 1 million = 16 million ounces).

If sold at a current wholesale price for $2,250 per ounce we have **$36,000,000,000 THAT'S OVER $36 BILLION PROFIT PER YEAR AND THAT'S JUST FOR COCAINE!!** If sold at retail for $100 per gram the gross sales are **$45.2 BILLION PER YEAR.**

Another incredible example is that of heroin. The DEA estimates that the actual cost per shot of heroin is about **twenty cents** to manufacture and import. This compares to a current street cost of **over $100.** Contrary to popular myth, many heroin addicts and users are functioning members of society with jobs, homes, and families. These people would be expected to continue paying the existing street cost that they are currently paying to the drug pushers. With the low cost of manufacture for heroin, we could easily provide the drug at cost to those that are currently forced to commit crimes to support their habit. Rather than commit an armed robbery to support a habit, a government subsidized addict could pay for his habit through working in soup kitchens, eliminating graffiti, or by performing other socially redeeming work.

The minority, those that are social misfits due to their addiction, should be helped to become productive. When they begin earning a decent salary, assuming they choose to continue using drugs, they will begin paying the going rate. Society benefits by adding another productive citizen. If the drug user decides to take advantage of a treatment program and quit using drugs, society also benefits because his criminal activity has stopped and he has become a useful taxpaying citizen.

Being the supplier of an addict's drugs puts the supplier in an incredible position of power to motivate the user. If an addict is able to put forth the effort to rob or steal, what sort of alternate and productive activity could we redirect this energy toward? Constructing low cost housing? Street clean up? Turning a weed lot into a baseball diamond? Let your imagination be your guide.

It only costs us twenty cents and we can ask for one hundred dollars worth of work, because that is what the addict would have had to pay his pusher. If he needs two shots a day we can certainly ask for eight hours worth of community enhancing effort in exchange for his fixes. OUR COST FOR THIS EFFORT WILL BE FORTY CENTS! Eight hours of work, even if halfhearted, is quite a bargain for forty cents.

The DEA estimates that total drug sales in the U.S. are now over **$110 billion per year.** Even if we allow an unbelievably high estimate of $10 billion in acquisition, distribution, and giveaway costs for the unemployed addicts, **THE DRUG SOLUTION** still provides the government with **$100 billion in new revenue without any new taxes or costs.** A good case can be made for the fact that we will have no distribution costs since we currently confiscate 10% of the drugs through our interdiction programs. This will not be the case with **THE DRUG SOLUTION** in force. This is the simplest, least painful solution to our deficit ever proposed. And we haven't even begun to discuss the additional benefits and advantages of **THE DRUG SOLUTION.**

Over a 5 year period we would raise nearly <u>$500 BILLION IN NEW REVENUE.</u> What could our country do with such a vast new source of revenue? Virtually every one of the problems of our country mentioned in the beginning of this chapter could be solved by implementing this program.

THE PLAN

We will implement this plan in three phases. The first, and most critical phase, is the formulating, writing and passage of the bill to make **THE DRUG SOLUTION** the law of the land. This is described in further detail in Chapter Ten.

Once the law has been passed, initial distribution will be accomplished directly through DEA offices. Recently confiscated contraband will be utilized as an initial supply and income source. During this transitional period, we will temporarily discontinue enforcement of drug laws, thus freeing our law enforcement personnel to enforce more serious crimes. We will temporarily allow pushers to continue to ply their trade. Drug sales will still be illegal but laws will be loosely enforced. This will put drug pushers on notice that their income source will soon be gone and that they might want to seek other means of employment. This will insure that we have a smooth transition to the new program and that spot shortages don't cause panic among addicts.

During the second phase pharmacies, liquor stores, or any approved retail outlet will be licensed to distribute the drugs Thus the profits will gradually transfer to legitimate small businesses, allowing for increased growth, profit, and employment. Licensing will be accomplished through the **BUREAU OF ALCOHOL, TOBACCO, AND FIREARMS.** They already have the knowledge and expertise to license controlled substances due to their experience with distributing licenses for alcoholic beverages. The procedure will be essentially the same.

The government will offer a 20% commission to the retailer that elects to join the program. This is much better than the profit realized by most items sold by such establishments.

During phase three we will resume strict enforcement of the laws against drug sales by non-authorized persons. The plan will be fully implemented. Distribution networks will be in place. Arrests will be quite minimal since the drugs will be readily available through authorized distributors and purchase from street vendors will carry the same harsh penalties we have now.

WHY WOULDN'T DRUG DEALERS KEEP ON SELLING?

Existing laws against the purchase and sale of drugs from unauthorized sources would remain in tact. The risk of buying or selling would then be too great to be worthwhile for either the seller or the buyer. Why would a drug user buy from a street vendor, and risk a felony conviction, when he could go buy government regulated drugs locally, without risk, and for the same price he has always paid? The testing and consistent quality of drugs from governmental sources would be an additional incentive to purchase from authorized sources.

The only advantage a street pusher could offer would be to undercut price. Where would he get his drugs? His former suppliers would be nonexistent because they would either be authorized, through foreign governments, or they would be out of business.

AN EXAMPLE OF HOW THE PROGRAM WOULD WORK

Let's take a simple example: Assume for a moment that we have passed the new law required to implement **THE DRUG SOLUTION.** We have progressed to phase three, and the plan is fully in place.

Joe Doaks, a pharmacist, in San Diego applied for and received a license to distribute cocaine. He subsequently places an order for one ounce of cocaine (28.3 grams) for $2,250 which he then sells at the current rate of $100 per gram or $2,830 for the whole ounce. This is a profit to the retailer of $580. This represents his 20% commission which he keeps. This is also **new profit and sales** which generate new sales and income taxes, further benefitting state, local and federal governments.

More importantly, the DEA acquired this ounce of cocaine at a cost of well under $200, thus leaving the DEA with a $2,000 profit. These profits are then forwarded to Washington to be used for the benefit of the country.

When we multiply this transaction by the thousands of transactions currently going on throughout the country, we will wind up with a minimum of **$100 billion in new revenue to the government and very likely a great deal more.**

In our example the pharmacist has placed his order via an "800" phone number to the Drug Enforcement Administration office in San Diego County. A DEA agent subsequently verifies the license and address of the pharmacy, prepares an invoice, and notifies a central warehouse to ship the ounce of cocaine. The product is then shipped via express mail to the retail store with signature of the licensee required. This will insure delivery to authorized personnel only. The DEA management will also be charged with setting prices as they already have the field knowledge and are aware of current prices, weight breakdowns, and demand requirements.

Naturally sales to minors will still be illegal, and certain restrictive laws such as driving under the influence will continue to be enforced, but most of these laws already exist. We simply continue enforcing these laws with our new streamlined and efficient law enforcement system. We would be more effective in reducing drug use by underage individuals because the street sources would cease to exist. Any minor can tell you that it's easier in today's climate to buy illicit drugs than alcohol. So it is safe to assume that our sample pharmacist will do everything possible to protect his valuable new license and not sell the cocaine to a minor.

A very important point is that law enforcement officials, relieved of the task of drug enforcement, would be free to address other forms of crime that are now drastically under enforced. Our newly unburdened police force can use the new time resource to enforce laws against drug sales to minors. It should begin to become obvious that the benefits of this plan are cumulative and tremendously beneficial to our society.

It should be noted that this concept will seem alarming to many Americans. These fears are understandable but they have their roots in emotions, not logic. We, as a country, must realize:

**THE ILLICIT DRUGS ARE BEING PUR-
CHASED NOW. THEY WILL CONTINUE
TO BE SOLD AND THERE IS NOTHING
WE CAN DO ABOUT IT. OUR ONLY
DECISION IS WHO WE WISH TO BENEFIT
FROM THE PROFITS OF THE SALES —
THE DRUG CARTELS AND GANGS OR
THE UNITED STATES GOVERNMENT
AND INEVITABLY, OURSELVES AND
OUR CHILDREN.**

It sounds almost silly to imagine the DEA actually acquiring and selling what are now illegal drugs, but it is critical that we understand
not only the benefits that we could realize by
implementing this plan but the disastrous
results of the status quo. Our current methods
show a catastrophic pattern: over 75 years, of
abject failure. We no longer have the luxury of
wasting billions of dollars per year while our
society is going broke. Our ineffective efforts
at enforcing the war on drugs can only be
described as a luxury. It is a huge expense for
something that is making no progress in solving the problem.

This type of thinking requires a significant adjustment to our normal patterns of thought. We
have been so brainwashed into looking at drugs
as an unsolvable problem, that a new way of
looking at and resolving it seems totally
foreign.

The United States is the largest and most
powerful nation on Earth. If we have the gumption to implement this plan, the world will follow.

The U.S. will always be the biggest beneficiary
to this plan, due to the simple fact that we are

the largest consumers of drugs in the world. Over 55% of all illicit drugs in the world wind up in the United States.

If we look logically at **THE DRUG SOLUTION** it is simple, effective, and unbelievably profitable. With the massive profits generated we can begin to address some of the very significant problems of our times. **REMEMBER, OVER $185 BILLION DOLLARS A YEAR ARE SPENT ON THE PURCHASE OF, AND ATTEMPTS TO CONTROL, ILLICIT DRUGS.**

HOW MUCH IS A BILLION?

Thirty years ago taxpayers would be shocked if a politician said that a given program would cost a million dollars. That sounded like a huge amount of money. Today our leaders throw the word billions around like they were so many match sticks. Let's put the problem into perspective by examining some examples of what all these billions mean.

A billion dollars, in one hundred dollar bills stacked neatly, will top the Empire State Building **NOT ONCE BUT TWICE!**

A billion dollars laid end to end will reach all the way around the world **NOT ONCE BUT FOUR TIMES!**

If you had **a million dollars** and spent $1,000 per day you would be broke in under three years.

If you had **a billion dollars** and spent one thousand dollars a day you would run out of money in the year **4730 AD!** That's 2,737 years from now!

The suggestions in this chapter show how we can start using some of these vast resources to the betterment of our country.

Chapter

Eight

*THE GREAT MASSES OF PEOPLE
WILL MORE EASILY FALL
VICTIMS TO A BIG LIE THAN A
SMALL ONE.*

ADOLPH   HITLER

Mein Kampf
1933

"BUT WE'LL BE A NATION OF DRUG ADDICTS"

THE DRUG SOLUTION is not, currently, a popular answer to the various crises in this country.

PRESIDENT BILL CLINTON responded to a call for drug legalization, by Attorney General Jocelyn Elders recently. He was quoted as saying "If drugs were legal my brother would be dead". **THE PRESIDENT WAS WRONG!** His brother is not dead because **HE DECIDED NOT TO KILL HIMSELF.** Regardless of where he lives, or what his situation, he could easily have found drugs in any city in this country. It is not the laws against drugs that saves or destroys lives, it is the individual choice of whether or not to use them and to what extent.

According to a 1989 Gallup poll, 90 percent of respondents opposed "legalization", 51 percent feared an increase in usage, and 64 percent were not convinced that organized crime would be eliminated should drugs be "legalized". This proposal does not suggest the legalization of drugs, in the sense that they would no longer be controlled, but rather suggests that the profits from the **inevitable** sales of the drugs be redirected toward positive uses. While no poll has been conducted on the unique proposals suggested in this plan, we can safely assume that a major effort towards educating the public on the details is necessary.

The single most frequently raised objection to a call to legalize drugs seems to be that if we legalize drugs everyone will start using them. This argument, if analyzed logically, is spurious and flies in the face of the facts. The fact is that the vast majority of the American people have no desire to use drugs, legal or not. Less than 1/3 of the public have ever even tried drugs. Around 12% are current users and about 1% are drug addicts. These statistics have remained remarkably consistent with or without the efforts of laws, enforcement agencies, and over 41 government organizations all attempting to eradicate drug use.

If 33% of the public has tried drugs and only 1% continue to abuse drugs then it should be obvious that the vast majority of people that experiment with drugs will not abuse them whether they are legally obtained or not.

A recent survey of recovering cocaine addicts indicates that 21% quit for health reasons, 12% were pressured by family and an additional 12% quit due to the cost of the drug. **Very few people are dissuaded from drug use simply because they are illegal.**

Take yourself, your family and friends, as an example. If, beginning tomorrow, you could go to a government store or pharmacy and purchase cocaine, would you begin using it? The answer for eighty five percent or more of the public is an emphatic NO! This remains true throughout society. The majority of our population would not use drugs under any circumstances but for some reason they believe that if drugs became legally obtainable everyone else would suddenly become a depraved addict! It is simply not logical to make these assumptions. The arguments most people use against drug use are very valid. Seventy to eighty percent of our citizens don't currently use drugs for the very good reason that they may eventually ruin your personal life, health, or may kill you. We also have any number of legitimate moral and ethical reasons for not getting involved with them.

The fact we must acknowledge is that the people in this country who choose to use drugs are already using them. Some are addicts, most are recreational or occasional users. Upon implementation of this plan, we will still have the same number of addicts we have now. We must come to terms with the fact that each individual will decide, for himself, to what extent he is going to use mind altering substances.

We don't have the ability or right to dictate the behavior of others until it has a direct impact on us. If we make laws to restrict a behavior, and that behavior is practiced by 25 to 30% of the public, we will be unable to enforce those laws no matter how hard we try or how much we spend. We will run out of money before we can arrest and punish the transgressors. Further, having these laws on our books and attempting to enforce them sabotages the respect we traditionally have toward law enforcement, thereby eroding our basic social fabric.

Ninety-nine percent of our population either elects not to use drugs or decides to limit the quantity they use before it causes significant damage to health, income, or lifestyle. About 1% of the population abuse these substances, and probably always will. This will remain true after **THE DRUG SOLUTION** becomes a reality.

If we implement **THE DRUG SOLUTION** we will, at least, have the funds needed to treat those abusers if, and when, **THEY DECIDE** that they would like to straighten out their lives. Even if the number of addicts were to double due to legalization (and that won't happen), we would still benefit tremendously as a society due to the related financial and social advantages gained.

We must be responsible enough to realize that providing services to addicts that wish to recover is a desireable objective. With the revenues from drug sales redirected to the government, we will be in a much better position to accomplish this objective. The point is that our current fiscal situation inhibits us from providing adequate services to those wishing to recover, thus compounding the problem.

We would, of course, be faced with the dichotomy of selling a product for profit on the one hand, and trying to cure the addicts on the other. We should be well prepared for dealing with this problem due to the fact that this is exactly what we do with alcohol and tobacco today! The reality, however, is that we will probably never totally eliminate the desire for mind and mood altering drugs, so we will always have this program as a substantial revenue source. It certainly seems that we, as a nation, would be better off if this revenue was in the hands of government and small businessmen than in the hands of organized crime, street gangs, and drug cartels.

LET'S TALK ABOUT HYPOCRISY

No discussion on drug law reform would be complete without exploring the hypocrisy of outlawing some psychoactive substances while permitting the use of others. In most cases, the drugs we allow are much worse than the ones we outlaw. This refers, of course, primarily to alcohol and tobacco. If someone were to propose that we begin importing a new substance into the United States that would give us a great new revenue source, one that would net millions to retailers, create new industries and jobs, we would probably be in favor of the new product. If we were then to learn that the product would kill 350,000 Americans per year, cause birth defects, make addicts out of most users, and wind up costing $65 billion per year in lost productivity and related health problems we would violently oppose the proposition. This is an accurate representation of the cost of cigarettes to our society.

Cigarettes, are the undisputed leader as a preventable cause of death in the U.S. Over 300,000 people die as a result of cigarette smoking every year. Recent studies indicate an additional 50,000 deaths are attributable to second hand smoke. Out of 100 regular smokers in this country one will die from murder, two will die in traffic accidents, and 25 will die from tobacco use. None will die from marijuana use. Eighty-five percent of all lung cancer deaths and thirty percent of all other cancer deaths are attributed to cigarette smoking. Where is the logic in outlawing marijuana, for example, when we allow the use of cigarettes? The answer is simple economics. We allow the sale of cigarettes because we don't want to give up the millions of tax dollars and other revenue generated by the sale of cigarettes. We have no intention of destroying an industry that generates so many jobs, but we never stop to think that the same potential exists for all other drugs.

Alcohol is another sanctioned drug that causes tremendous problems and costs for our society. We have decided, through a very painful learning process, that we are better off as a society in keeping alcohol legal than in trying to outlaw it. Prohibition during the 1920's was singularly ineffective in reducing the availability of alcohol to the public. The prohibition laws resulted in providing an income source for organized crime, thus allowing it to gain a foothold in this country. This is a perfect example of the foolishness of prohibiting any desired substance. Since we could not enforce the prohibition laws, we eventually legalized alcohol once again. The result was the creation of a huge, legal, job creating, tax producing industry that was no longer supporting organized crime.

Our choice is basically the same for drugs today as it was for alcohol seventy years ago. Shouldn't we learn from our past mistakes and start benefitting from the drug sales that are inevitably going to take place regardless of our enforcement efforts?

If we combined every form of death and destruction caused by what we now classify as illegal drugs, and compared them with the negative impact of legal drugs, the problems created by illegal drugs would not even scratch the surface of the damage from legal drugs. Cigarettes and alcohol alone cause massively more social damage than all illegal drugs combined.

The primary cause of problems with illegal drugs result from the fact that they are illegal. Drug related crime and violence would be eliminated or drastically reduced if were to implement **THE DRUG SOLUTION.** If drugs are available from retail outlets the drug users will buy and use their drug of choice in relative peace.

If we are not going legalize drugs, and we are to be consistent, then we must stop being hypocrites and outlaw cigarettes, alcohol, soda drinks containing caffeine, coffee, most cold remedies, NO-DOZ and literally hundreds of other products in common use. This idea is ridiculous but no more ridiculous than our current hypocritical, inconsistent, and unenforceable laws against drug use.

Yet another example of the futility of attempting to control individual behavior is that of gambling. For decades we, as a society tried to outlaw gambling in all but a few remote select locations. Today gambling is a major source of revenue for most state governments. It has been a tremendous income source for the California school system for example. Without the income from the state lottery the school system would be bankrupt. If we can turn that which we used to call a horrible negative into a meaningful positive, why not do the same with drug sales?

THE MORAL DILEMMA

Another aspect of any attempt to revise our drug laws is that of the moral concerns. If we implement **THE DRUG SOLUTION** are we giving tacit approval to drug use? The fact is that **IT DOESN'T MATTER!** Whether we are saying drug use is good or bad is irrelevant. The people who choose to use drugs have already made their moral choices and the rest of us have no ability, right, or obligation to try to change that. Are we giving approval to use cigarettes or alcohol because they are legal? No. We are allowing individuals to choose for themselves whether they are going to use these products. We, as a society, should provide treatment for those individuals wishing to change and financially unable to secure treatment for themselves. Beyond that, any attempts to force our moral dictates on another will prove completely ineffective.

Drug users and drug abusers should be considered exactly the same as social drinkers or alcoholic's. Anyone with experience in dealing with an alcoholic knows that there is virtually nothing anyone can do or say to influence the alcoholics behavior until he makes the conscious decision that he must do something to change. Go to any meeting of Alcoholics Anonymous or any drug clinic and ask someone who is recovering if he could have been talked out of the behavior prior to his "hitting bottom". The answer will be an emphatic NO!

We may look at the individual with dismay or disdain, but our recriminations have little or no effect on the individual's actions. Moral judgement, or criticism may even compound the likelihood of the undesired activity. We must realize that we have very little control over the action of an individual that is not harming anyone but himself.

We must also consider the fact that our current laws give tacit approval to the activities of organized crime, gangs, and drug cartels. Because we are unwilling or unable to stop illegal drug sales we are indirectly supporting these groups.

Everyone would like to see a world in which we were all so comfortable and secure with ourselves that mind altering substances were completely unnecessary, but we are a long way from this objective. It is the height of folly to let our wishful thinking blind us to reality. We must do some serious self appraisal of our national objectives. On one hand we can continue pontificating and finger pointing. We can keep up our show of moral high ground by telling the world how hard we are trying to curb drug use, but what is the cost of maintaining this course? We won't eliminate drug use. Seventy-five years and billions of dollars have been spent trying to eradicate them with no success. We will continue supporting the worst criminals in our society and we won't benefit from any of the social improvements discussed in the next chapter. When coupled with the fact that we can never win, is the drug war worth this tremendous price?

Our decision is not, "Shall we accept drug use." It is "Who gets the profits and what is to be done with them". This is not a program of legalization so much as it is a program of taxation and the subsequent tremendous social reform that could be realized by using those taxes for the betterment of our country. Drug use exists and will continue to exist no matter how much we wish it would go away. We may as well start benefitting from the inevitable.

Chapter

Nine

SOCIAL BENEFITS

Let's examine some of the profound changes the this program could offer our country.

ELIMINATE THE DEFICIT

One of the greatest problems and concerns in this country today is our federal deficit. The deficit, more than any other factor, threatens the long term future and security of this country.

One dilemma we face is that the people of this country are at their taxable limit. Every news program, talk show and newspaper article is loaded with indications that we citizens simply refuse to pay any additional taxes. The message is clear, "Cut spending, no new taxes".

Our education system is crying for more money, cities and counties are forced to cut police and fire services. Federal and state agencies realize this, and are attempting to cut back on services thus earning the wrath of the public.

A recent complaint by our state politicians is that "unfunded mandates" are bankrupting our state economies. An unfunded mandate is a requirement that a state fulfill certain obligations, such as the clean air act, but they are provided no federal funds with which to accomplish this. This is one of the ploys that Congress has used to accomplish an objective without having to come up with the money to pay for it.

Another example is that of the state of California, which has siphoned off property taxes that, at one time, were shared with the cities and counties. The cities and counties used to count on 50% of all property tax revenue. This has shrunk to 15%, and has caused a near revolt in local government. Some counties are simply refusing to pay.

The common citizen is under the impression that, at this tax rate, and with a one and a half trillion dollar budget a year, we should be getting more, not less, in the way of services. At every turn the American public feels the pinch of yet another nickel and dime tax, from radically increased vehicle registration costs to additional sales and gasoline taxes. The publics heels are dug in. The "READ MY LIPS NO NEW TAXES" broken promise may have lost the election for George Bush. Many citizens have adopted the questionable habit of simply voting no on any tax increase even if it sounds like a good idea. The public feels impotent because the deficit just keeps getting bigger. Politicians just don't to get the picture; the public won't pay anymore taxes. President Clinton is now losing popularity because he is proposing increased taxes without reducing the deficit.

THE DRUG SOLUTION will eliminate the deficit with **NO NEW TAXES.** We will instantly have an increase in revenue of over **$185 billion each and every year.** Even a tax and spend administration would have trouble getting rid of this amount of money without eliminating the federal deficit over the next four years.

The federal deficit for 1992 was $277 billion **THE DRUG SOLUTION PROVIDES REVENUE SOURCES AND COST REDUCTIONS TO <u>CUT THE DEFICIT IN HALF IMMEDIATELY.</u>** When coupled with the proposed reductions in spending in the 1993 budget, we have **ENTIRELY ELIMINATED THE FEDERAL DEFICIT IN ONE YEAR**. A simple solution to our deficit would be to mandate all profits generated from drug sales go directly towards the reduction of the deficit until it no longer exists. We also have literally hundreds of hidden benefits by the implementation of this plan.

A PERMANENT SOLUTION TO PRISON OVERCROWDING

We could, in fact, solve our prison overcrowding emergency in very short order. All that would be required is to release, on parole, every criminal who has been convicted solely on nonviolent drug possession and selling charges. As mentioned earlier, 58% of the people currently incarcerated in our federal, state, and local facilities, have been convicted solely on nonviolent drug related offenses. This would immediately free up 300,000 prison and jail cells. We would immediately solve our prison crisis. And we would have plenty of room to house all violent criminals for very long sentences.

We would not eliminate the laws against sales and distribution of these illicit drugs. We would simply grant a one time amnesty to those currently in prison. An exception to our current drug laws will be granted duly licensed distributors that have met, and continue to meet our criteria thus obtaining a license similar to a liquor license. These drug licenses, incidently, provide yet another new revenue source.

Future criminals convicted of selling untaxed drugs without being licensed will be dealt with harshly. We will have the prison space, unburdened police department, and efficient court system to deal with them in a much more efficient manner. We will immediately remove the desperate need for new $50 billion in new prisons, eliminate the $15 billion currently being spent on housing these criminals, and, in all likelihood, 90% of these former felons will not repeat their crime for the simple reason that they will no longer have any customers.

A SOLUTION FOR OUR SMALL FARMERS?

Such a large number of prisoners, suddenly released on society, also causes a few problems. The logistics of releasing 300,000 individuals with questionable backgrounds is a reasonable cause for concern. Why not offer exiting prisoners a job? Select farms that have opted to join the "**The Small Farmers Subsidy Exchange Program**" would be provided with a labor source, and permission to raise various drug related crops. Small farmers have been extremely vocal about to the need for government subsidies and financial aid in recent years.

In exchange for existing subsidies, select farms would be allowed to grow, marijuana, coca plants, and opium poppies to be refined into a percentage of the various drugs demanded by users. These crops would be planted on land that we are currently paying farmers not to grow anything on. Exiting prisoners released due to the drug amnesty program, could be offered positions as farm workers to help raise these crops. These positions could be relatively high paying due to the high profits generated by the crops in comparison to those normally earned by small farmers. Any prison guards, displaced due to lower inmate populations will be transferred to the farms to keep order and insure compliance with distribution laws. Processing and refining will take place in other locations to preclude any black market activity.

This aspect of the program would generate a number of benefits; The immediate employment of large numbers of prisoners would provide an obvious opportunity for these individuals to become part of the mainstream. They would be reintroduced to the idea of hard work for good pay. Those that choose to continue their old habits of drug use, could be provided drugs as partial compensation for their labor. We would begin to generate at least some of our own product. This would reduce the possibility of a cartel being formed in the future that would control and drive up the wholesale prices of the drugs from foreign countries.

There are about 250,000 farms in the U.S. if 20% of the farms participate in this program, we would average 5 parolees per farm to provide the labor for the new crops. Farmers that elect to take advantage of this program would have a tremendous cash crop, and subsequent profits. The profit per acre for these crops are much higher than for standard crops. More profit means increased tax revenues. High cost farm machinery would not be required. Instead the efforts of the released prisoners would provide the required labor.

The jobs could be offered based on a prisoner's guarantee of good conduct while on the farm. Subsequent unacceptable behavior would result in a return to prison, or simple termination depending on the behavior. Marijuana, for example, has not only a tremendous profit potential for drug sales, but it produces seven times the fiber per acre as comparable crops. Fiber is needed for the production of such products as paper, textiles, rope, and fabrics. It has further value for medicinal uses for glaucoma, which causes 15% of the blindness in this country, and treatment of those suffering from the nausea caused by chemo-therapy.

Perhaps we can even placate some of the environmentalists by growing and harvesting marijuana as a fiber source thereby reducing the need for timber harvesting.

An additional benefit from the growing of marijuana is the production of hemp oil. Recent research indicates that hemp oil is a viable alternative fuel for diesel powered vehicles and can be refined into a clean burning methanol source. Could this help us to reduce our dependence on foreign oil?

A JOB FOR EVERYONE

Another major concern in this country is that of employment. If any one worry is constant among the citizens of this country, it is that of becoming jobless or, for those already unemployed, finding a new job. Many surveys indicate that the economy and the deficit are our major cause of distress. This is true, but the major reason behind those concerns are maintaining or regaining employment.

Many of our unskilled and semi-skilled jobs have moved, and continue to move to Mexico, Asia, and the Pacific rim. The primary reason behind this exodus is the fact that the United States has become too expensive. The largest single cost item in building a car, for example is health care. A major financial stimulus package is crucial to our future in order to keep jobs here and to create new employment opportunities.

We must not only provide acceptable good paying jobs to our inner city youth, but to every man and woman in the country who wishes to work and better themselves. We must stabilize our economy so that employers no longer find it necessary to go outside the United States to manufacture their products. Finances, once again, are the hurdle that we must overcome.

The tremendous increase in revenues provided for in this plan, will allow for a number of factors that will drastically reduce unemployment in this country.

Once our deficit has been eliminated, the additional income generated by this plan will be used to implement job-creating and training programs that are currently not affordable due to budget restrictions. It is worth noting that the elimination of the deficit itself will have a tremendously positive benefit to the confidence of the country. This confidence will be demonstrated by increased spending by both business and individuals. This stimulus will, of itself, increase employment. President

Clinton's Job Creation Bill was recently defeated primarily because the Republican senators resisted a multi-billion dollar new expense with no funds to pay for it. Upon implementation of **THE DRUG SOLUTION** we could easily afford programs like HEADSTART, and a much larger summer jobs program.

As mentioned earlier, many small businesses would also benefit directly from the sales of the drugs via various licensed retail outlets. This increase in sales and profits allows for the hiring of additional employees. How many companies and local governments have imposed hiring freezes due to the poor economy and a lack of faith in our country's ability to recover? This program will quickly alleviate these concerns.

A small percentage of our newfound profits could completely revitalize the **Small Business Administration**, thereby providing loan guarantees and assistance for new and expanding small businesses that provide the majority of new jobs in this country.

THE RETURN OF THE NUCLEAR FAMILY

The nuclear, or two parent, family has been eroded in this country due to our tenancy to accept the unacceptable. Over the last thirty years we have begun to accept the actions of those who father children and then walk away. This shows a complete lack of responsibility and deteriorates our basic values. There is an underlying cause behind this behavior. The scenarios mentioned in chapter six eluded to the lack of self esteem plaguing minorities and inner city youth. This lack of confidence, compounded by the inability to find suitable employment, has caused a sense of hopelessness among these groups. It is natural and normal for a well adjusted, confident individual to love, provide for, and nurture his family. As **THE DRUG SOLUTION** begins to have positive effects on the economy, jobs will become available. The old cycle of dropping out of school to become a drug dealer, and the inevitable subsequent prison sentences and lifelong unemployment will be broken. Gradually self respect, employment, income, and responsibility will return to these individuals. This increase in personal value will encourage responsibility for family and community. It will also greatly reduce violent crime. People who respect themselves respect the rights of others.

The welfare system, as it currently exists, also subsidizes and encourages illegitimacy and the break up of the two parent family. The current movement to provide jobs for single parents must be encouraged, but **THE DRUG SOLUTION** will be the primary catalyst for resolving this critical issue.

PUTTING ORGANIZED CRIME OUT OF BUSINESS

Organized crime is an enterprise involving a number of persons in close social interaction, whose purpose is to secure profit and power by engaging in illegal (and legal) activities. The organization avoids competition and strives to control particular activities on an industrial or territorial basis. There is a willingness to use violence, bribery, blackmail or a combination of the three achieve ends or to maintain discipline.

Groups worldwide that have been identified as being involved in organized criminal activity include Japanese yakuza, Chinese triads, Neapolitan Camorra, Sicilian MAFIA, and Colombian and Mexican crime "families." In the United States they include Italian-American crime "families," outlaw motorcycle gangs like the Hell's Angels, and a variety of black, white, Asian and Latin gangs. Organized crime in the United States dates back to the prohibition period (1920-33) when the ban on alcoholic beverages led criminals to form large scale syndicates to run and protect bootlegging enterprises. It is incredible to realize that in effect, **PROHIBITION CAUSED ORGANIZED CRIME** in the U.S. When prohibition ended, some of these syndicates moved into other forms of criminal activity, including labor racketeering, loan sharking, gambling, and drug trafficking. Organized crime currently has four primary sources of illegal income in this country: illegal drugs, and illegal gambling, prostitution, and extortion. Drugs and gambling are their largest sources of income. Illegal drugs sales represent over 80% of the income for all crime syndicates.

Law enforcement efforts against organized crime are limited by the constraints placed on government in a democratic society and by the secrecy to which criminals are sworn. The U.S. has legislation specifically designed to deal with organized crime and improved federal law enforcement resources have resulted in many successful prosecutions of persons in organized crime.

The implementation of **THE DRUG SOLU-TION** would, in a very short time, cripple or destroy the primary income source for these organizations. This could virtually put them out of business. Income from gambling has already been eroded because many states, hungry for additional revenues, have implemented legalized gambling in the form of casinos, state lotteries, keno machines, and card rooms.

ELIMINATE GANGS AND GANG VIOLENCE

A more recent, and perhaps more worrisome, phenomenon than that of organized crime is the increasing power and ruthless behavior of street gangs. Not an inner city in America is free from their fearsome tactics. Drive-by shootings muggings, rape and gang wars are but a few of the activities of these criminals. These thugs are highly dependent on illegal drugs sales as a source of income.

Without the income from drug sales, where does a gang member get the vehicle for the drive by shooting? The gas for the vehicle? The weapon? The only option left to the gang member is to steal these things. But remember we would now have law enforcement agencies that are streamlined, efficient, and work to enforce laws against burglaries, robberies, and other crimes against individuals and businesses.

Implementation of **THE DRUG SOLUTION** not only eliminates the primary income source for most street gangs, but it has the added benefit of freeing law enforcement agencies from the task of enforcing drug laws. Police and federal agencies that are currently wasting vast resources in an attempt to control these corrupt groups, will be assigned to more urgent duties and tasks.

Sixty percent of the activity of law enforcement currently goes toward enforcing drug laws, and drug related crimes. That same sixty percent would be reassigned to making life miserable for those street gangs that elect to continue a criminal lifestyle.

We would also have a streamlined prison and court system. It will easily deal with, and incarcerate any criminals foolish enough to continue a life of crime. Remember that as much as 70% of our total law enforcement, judicial, and prison resources currently go towards drug enforcement efforts.

The problem today is that **CRIME PAYS.** Twenty years ago nearly 100% of bank robbers were brought to justice. If you robbed a bank you would probably go to jail and serve a long sentence.

Today 55% of bank robberies go unsolved. What's worse, those that are caught usually serve **under three years in prison**. Due to prison overcrowding, criminals no longer have an incentive to stay away from crime. If you rob a bank and get $75,000 you have one in two chance of getting away with it. If you get caught, and serve a three year sentence you have still earned $25,000 per year tax free for robbing a bank. We need to get back to the days when it did not pay to be involved in criminal activity of any sort. Ask any police officer in the country how his duties would change if the drug enforcement equation was removed. He will tell you, to a man, that he could be much more effective in dealing with all the other aspects of crime.

We will still have the problem of drug crazed individuals, but this problem will certainly be no worse than it is today. If some individuals make a habit of this anti-social behavior we will have plenty of officers available to subdue them and plenty of prison space in which to incarcerate them. A perhaps more important point is that they will know a cell is waiting for them. They will be much more motivated to change their bad habits if they know that the revolving door in the prison system has stopped turning.

MAKE EVERY STREET IN THE NATION SAFE AGAIN

Another concern of Americans is that crime, in general, and violent crime in particular, has rendered many of our streets unsafe to walk. Millions of low income, elderly, and minorities, in this country run a significant risk when doing something as simple as going to the market. They live in constant fear of being shot, robbed or raped. The crime rate in the last three decades has risen consistently and is now out of control. How could we restore safety and security to every street in America?

It's difficult to imagine, but as little as 30 years ago, people didn't worry about walking the street at night. We left our doors unlocked. Children could play without fear. Our crime rate in general was not a major concern in this country. Did Beaver Cleaver ever have an episode in which Wally got mugged? Ridiculous! The concept was beyond our imagination. Was Penny ever raped in an episode of Sky King? Of course not! The possibility of these events were unthinkable, but watch any soap opera today and they will be rife with murder, rape, robbery, and burglary.

What changed? Illegal Drugs and our useless attempt to enforce the laws regarding them, caused our law enforcement officials to become spread too thin and thereby become less effective. No matter how many resources we throw at drug enforcement, we can't win because we are trying to enforce laws that are broken, at least occasionally, by one third of our country's population. We unwittingly allowed the criminal element, gangs and organized crime in particular, to gain a foothold. They subsequently capitalized on the profits to be gained and grew more powerful. In essence these unenforceable laws against drugs caused crime to become a very profitable venture. This set up a vicious cycle that has lead to a loss of respect, in some quarters, for our laws and our officers.

Just watch an episode of "COPS" and you will see criminals that fail to yield to a police officer's demands to stop or pull over. They often blatantly lie to the officers, and perhaps most worrisome, they consider a felony arrest to be a minor inconvenience. This attitude is due to a number of factors all of which are related, directly or indirectly, to our useless, ineffective attempt at prohibition of the use of illegal drugs.

Gang activity and drive by shootings, for example, are an everyday occurrence in most inner cities of the U.S. Most of these shootings are turf related and turf is, in large part, protected drug territory. The money generated by illicit drug sales are, to a large extent, used to support these gangs. While the police are engaged trying to curtail these activities, they are unavailable to reduce and solve an unprecedented number of rape, robbery, burglary, and murder cases. We simply don't have the manpower or financial resources to do it all. What would happen if some of this money were removed from the street and reallocated, by government, into educational programs and job creation in our inner cities? As in many cases. the benefits of **THE DRUG SOLUTION,** and results of its implementation, are cumulative.

First, the gang members would no longer have their source of income. Second, the same funds that are used to support these felons could now be used to educate and employ them. What if we were to employ gangs with some of these funds at say ten dollars an hour removing graffiti and trash from inner city streets? Gangs of themselves are not bad. They are just groups of people. The illegal activity associated with the gang members is the problem. It is not beyond reason to imagine one gang competing against another for contracts to clean up our streets, rebuilding abandoned housing, or any number of other positive tasks. **All we need is the money to provide the incentive. We get the money from the sale of the drugs that are causing the problem now.**

Law enforcement agencies throughout the nation would benefit in the billions due to the fact that efforts to enforce drug laws would be unnecessary. This would, of course, free up overburdened agencies thus allowing them to concentrate on the various remaining criminals. These criminals would soon be caught and incarcerated in our newly vacated prisons, for nice long sentences. Additional enforcement would lead inevitably to reduced crime. If an officer is not spending his time busting someone for drug possession, he may well be foiling a burglary, rape, or murder.

This theory was born out recently when, on the day the jury was to decide on the Rodney King case, every officer in Los Angeles was on duty along with a back up contingent of the national guard. This force was on duty to preclude a repeat of the L.A. riots which ensued as a result of the first not guilty findings of the officers involved. The result was a profound reduction in criminal activity. The criminals knew that they were more than matched if they attempted to stir up trouble, and the following days were among the quietest in recent memory.

Is this wishful thinking? Pie in the sky? A famous multi- millionaire was once quoted as saying **"IF WHAT YOU HAVE TO GAIN IS MUCH MORE THAN WHAT YOU HAVE TO LOSE, GIVE IT A TRY".** We have very little to lose since our laws are not working now. Seventy-five years of tremendous expense and effort have provided little or no benefits. What we have to gain is nothing less than the rebirth of our nation. The benefits, both direct and indirect of implementing this idea are nothing short of phenomenal.

Significant resistance to any such changes by the very criminals that stand to lose by implementing **THE DRUG SOLUTION** should be expected. Organized crime and drug cartels, in particular, have a history of violence when their sources of income are threatened. This history has been most evident in foreign countries such as Columbia where acts of violence reminiscent of terrorism have been common.

The counterbalance will, again, be the reduced demand on law enforcement. Eliminating the necessity of enforcement of drug laws will enable local law enforcement, the FBI, the DEA, and other agencies to redouble efforts in controlling the activities of these groups. This resistance will reduce gradually as the income of these organizations begin to dry up. The Columbian cartels had virtually unlimited funds with which to terrorize a very poor country. The United States, on the other hand, will instantly have massive resources and personnel with which to prevent these activities.

INCREASE ENTITLEMENT PAYMENTS BY 15%

A major concern of our senior citizens and low income individuals is that the federal government will yield to pressure to reduce what are referred to as "entitlement spending payments." Entitlement spending encompasses such monthly government payments to individuals as Social Security, Welfare, Food stamps, AFDC. and Medicare. The recipients of these funds have every right to be concerned. The fact is that without a major new source of revenue, these programs are doomed to be slowly whittled away by Washington until they amount to little or nothing. We no longer have the funds to continue to pay these benefits. The working public will not accept additional taxes to cover the increased costs. The lifespan of the average U.S. citizen is increasing. The number of working citizens to pay for these entitlements is decreasing. All indications are that Social Security will run out of money if we don't fund it with some type of alternate revenue source.

THE DRUG SOLUTION, once again, offers a method of unraveling a very difficult problem. With a portion of the profits generated by the sale of cocaine, marijuana, heroin, and other illicit drugs we could easily increase entitlement payments by 15% or more once our deficit has been eliminated.

Perhaps more important, the improved economy and increased employment opportunities provided by **THE DRUG SOLUTION** will offer a method for welfare recipients to get off the government dole and become social assets rather than liabilities.

Numerous additional social benefits could be realized. We could, for example, fund drug clinics and outpatient programs in an effort to rehabilitate current and future drug addicts wishing to improve their lives. This would turn a percentage of them into productive tax-paying citizens.

Our current treatment programs are drastically under funded, and they are ineffective. Anyone wishing to participate in these programs is put on a waiting list of 3 to 6 months. By the time the drug user is allowed into the program, his motivation has often evaporated. He finds himself stuck in the downward self- destructive spiral of addiction again. By reinvesting some of the money generated from the sales, we could provide the finest programs in the world for those individuals wishing to improve themselves. This is unquestionably the best method of reducing drug use in this country, and infinitely better than our current ineffective and costly efforts at repressing drug use.

PROVIDING A WORKABLE HEALTH CARE SYSTEM TO ALL

The Clinton administration has recently proposed a sweeping health care reform that most people would like to see implemented, except for on thing: IT COSTS TOO MUCH!! There is simply no way that we Americans can afford to buy health insurance for every person in the country. Where can we possibly find the $50 billion or more per year this program will require?

As you might have guessed by now, the tremendous income generated by **THE DRUG SOLUTION** provides us with the answer to yet another social dilemma. We could easily use some of this money to fund the new health care program. The first year of the new health care system could be completely financed just out of the money we have saved because we no longer have to spend $50 billion in building new prisons. We have estimated a conservative $100 billion per year in NET PROFIT generated by the sale of drugs alone. Related additional taxes, profits, and savings would bring in another $85 billion at a minimum.

Remember that this $100 billion estimate does not include an estimated $4 billion in savings to federal law enforcement, $8 billion in local law enforcement savings, $6 billion in reduced prosecution costs, $15.7 billion saved by releasing criminals convicted solely of drug offenses, and $50 billion in subsequent unnecessary construction of new prisons.

Imagine a health care system with the funds to continue offering our current unmatched quality of service to every man, woman, and child in the U.S. This type of program combines the desires of both political parties. It allows for the desire to spend for the benefit of all that is professed by the liberals It does not raise taxes in any way, shape, or form, thereby satisfying the desires of the fiscally conservative.

In this way we accomplish the best of both worlds and wind up with a nation that is in a much better position to move confidently into the next century.

ADEQUATE FUNDING FOR AIDS RESEARCH

Many Americans believe that we as a country have not provided adequate funding for research on the AIDS epidemic in our country. The primary reason behind this lack of funding is lack of funds. In an era when nearly all segments of government are being asked to scale back, AIDS research has been no exception A twofold effort at the control of this dangerous disease could be launched in conjunction with **THE DRUG SOLUTION.**

First, a major factor in the spreading of AIDS is through the sharing of drug paraphernalia such as needles. Sharing these devices spreads the disease, thus compounding the problem. The distribution of single use syringes at the distribution points would go a long way toward solving this aspect of the AIDS epidemic. Second, a small percentage of the new revenue generated from the sale of drugs could be directed toward AIDS research thus satisfying the demands of those requesting more efforts towards the eradication of this epidemic.

As promised in the introduction, the ideas in this book have offered realistic, achievable objectives that will: lower your taxes, eliminate the deficit, solve our prison and court overcrowding, provide additional employment, reduce crime, eradicate violence, and increase social benefits, all without raising taxes. We have touched on many of the social benefits that we can expect to gain as a result of implementing **THE DRUG SOLUTION**, but we have barely begun to elaborate on the secondary effects that this financial windfall would bring. As time goes on our improved economy and income will allow for many of the programs that are currently under funded. Revitalizing our schools, our roads and infrastructure, and space exploration, for example, will be among the countless social benefits we can expect over the long term. The ripple effect of this program will provide nothing short of a rebirth of our nation.

All that is required is the action of the American public in order to make these promises a reality.

Chapter

Ten

> *THE ONLY THING*
>
> *NECESSARY FOR THE*
>
> *TRIUMPH OF EVIL IS*
>
> *FOR GOOD MEN TO DO*
>
> NOTHING
> Edmund Burke

HOW TO MAKE "THE DRUG SOLUTION" A REALITY

We have a number of very real problems to overcome if we are to make **THE DRUG SOLUTION** a reality in the U.S. The first, and most significant, challenge is to educate the American public about the benefits of this program. While drug legalization has previously been proposed, the proposal suggested in this book has never been outlined or debated. The unique idea, of using the profits generated from illegal drug sales directly for social benefit and change, must be discussed and debated.

If, having read these ideas, you agree that it is time for a change, **YOU MUST HELP GET THE WORD OUT**. Send copies of **THE DRUG SOLUTION** to your friends and acquaintances. Discuss the ideas, weigh the pros and cons of the plan. Call or write your Senators and Congressmen. Ask them to review this book. Join **C.F.I.D.S.,** (described below). A major effort to educate the public book has begun. We are airing our views on talk shows, throughout the country, advertising on radio, TV, and in magazines. The best way to convince others is word of mouth. This is where your efforts are crucial.

"TIDTAD"

If, as we expect, the majority of the country sees the wisdom in implementing these ideas, the next step is to find a member of Congress willing to risk proposing a bill. Congress is well known for rhetoric and many members will probably jump at the chance to disparage **THE DRUG SOLUTION** in order to appear "honorable and upstanding representatives". We suggest that once we have found a representative with the gumption to propose the bill, we include a number of safeguards and concepts that will help it through Congress.

Let's call this bill **THE ILLICIT DRUG TAX AND DISTRIBUTION ACT.** This forms the acronym **TIDTAD.** First, in order to encourage congress to vote for this bill, **TIDTAD** will incorporate a major modification option to the congressional pay plan.

This option will be written to grant any member of the House or Senate an opportunity to participate in the benefits gained by implementing the plan. A Congressman would be reimbursed at a rate of .005% of the sales generated in his or her district. This would give an estimated average raise of **$114,000 A YEAR TO EVERY MEMBER OF THE HOUSE.** Senators would receive .0015% of the sales in his state or an average of **$150,000 TO EACH SENATOR.** This would represent a significant increase in income to the members of congress while representing a very small percentage of the new revenue. It will also help motivate our politicians to take a difficult stand towards making **THE DRUG SOLU-TION** a reality and will give the largest raises to the politicians with the largest problems in their respective areas. This plan would be optional so that any congressman that found the idea of a bonus for being involved with drug sales distasteful, could decline or donate the funds to drug rehabilitation centers that are located in his district or state.

A secondary provision of the Congressional Pay Plan Revision will be to grant a $100,000 per year raise to every member of Congress for every percentage point reduction in the annual budget. We will thereby motivate Congress to cut spending and gradually reduce our national debt.

Many people will have a major objection to these provisions of the bill. "Why on earth would we want to give a raise to the crooks in Washington?" Many will ask. "They already make too much and they probably steal more." This is a fair question and there are three parts to the answer. First, the increase in salary will be pennies when compared with the billions in benefits we will receive as a nation. The raise is a simple form of motivation to help convince our politicians to back the bill. Any politician in today's climate that would propose a bill like **TIDTAD** is risking his political career. This point is well worth the paltry pay increase we will grant Congress, if we can get the support needed to pass the bill. Second, we must remember the fact that **TIDTAD,** as described below, puts a permanent spending freeze on government. This may be overridden only with a two-thirds majority vote. Congress will never be able to muster a two-thirds majority unless we truly have an emergency. If we had passed a provision like this 15 years ago we would have no deficit today. Again what we have to gain is tremendously more important than giving Congress an insignificant pay raise. Third, with these raises in place, a position as a Senator or Congressmen becomes competitive with the salaries received by some of our large corporations. We may finally be able to attract some real talent to these positions and begin running this country in an intelligent business-like manner.

One factor that **must** be included in **TIDTAD** is that we impose **AN ACROSS THE BOARD PERMANENT SPENDING FREEZE**, on all government spending activity. This provision to the bill is absolutely crucial. In other words our government gets to benefit from the huge windfall represented by **TIDTAD** but **THAT'S'S IT!** No more spending! Congress has an insatiable appetite for income. The only way to curb this appetite is a spending freeze, and the only way to get a spending freeze past the special interest groups is to offer an irresistible "perk" that will be financed by **TIDTAD**. Remember that this bill, when fully implemented, will increase the country's net spendable income by well over **$185 BILLION PER YEAR.** Indirect additional benefits, as discussed earlier, would further benefit federal, state, and local budgets in the hundreds of billions of dollars. **TIDTAD** represents a much larger spending increase than has ever been proposed by the present or any other administration, **AND WE ACCOMPLISH IT WITHOUT ONE NEW TAX INCREASE.**

When coupled with the **ONE AND A HALF TRILLION DOLLAR ANNUAL INCOME** the government already spends, this should prove adequate for the foreseeable future. As a safeguard, a two-thirds majority vote of both houses will override this spending freeze.

190

Another aspect of the bill will be to form a committee to oversee the distribution of funds, set priorities for their use, and grant licenses to sell. A provision that the first 24 months profits be used exclusively for deficit reduction may prove to be our best investment for the initial income generated by this program. It will also prove to be a very strong argument in support of the bill.

The bill will further provide for the immediate parole of all convicted felons and the discharge of all pending court cases consisting **SOLELY OF CRIMES PERTAINING TO NON-VIOLENT DRUG OFFENSES.** Criminals with multiple convictions combining drug felonies and other related transgressions will serve out their term. We will now, thankfully have plenty of prison space to house them.

Upon the elimination of our deficit, we will set our priorities and subsequently incorporate, **JOBS AND TRAINING PROGRAMS ENTITLEMENT INCREASES, AND OTHER SOCIAL PROGRAMS,** as funding becomes available through continued sales.

We will also spell out the specifics of the redefinition of the Drug Enforcement Agency. It will be charged with coordinating importation and distribution of the various drugs.

The **Farmers Home Administration (FHA)** will be charged with the implementation of the farm employment program discussed earlier.

A further provision of **TIDTAD** will be to insure that nothing can or will be done to promote drug use. Advertising the sale of drugs in any form will be banned. Public service announcements will offer help for those that are willing to end the drug use lifestyle. We will have come terms with the fact that drug use is inevitable, but we will do nothing to encourage further consumption.

The usual debate and discussion on this bill as it works its way through Congress will insure that all aspects are covered and concerns are addressed. Our objective of a better overall situation in our country will be met.

C.F.I.D.S.

THE COMMITTEE FOR IMPLEMENTING THE DRUG SOLUTION

C.F.I.D.S. is a grass roots organization committed to making **THE DRUG SOLUTION** a reality. *C.F.I.D.S.* will operate only within the boundaries of current law and does not endorse the use of any mind altering, or psycho active substance, be it legal or illegal. We simply believe that the end product or profits of *inevitable* drug sales should be rerouted to more positive end uses. It is time for a change in our drug laws. It is time to stop supporting criminals and thieves and begin incarcerating them.

A national effort has been launched utilizing newspaper, radio, television, talk shows, and computer networks. We are committed to the ideas outlined in this book and are actively seeking like-minded individuals.

We believe that **THE DRUG SOLUTION** will solve most or all of the social ills facing our country. Should you have an interest in becoming a member of **C.F.I.D.S.**, please contact:

C.F.I.D.S.
c/o RFTI Publishing
PO BOX 651
PORTERVILLE, CA 93207
(800) 266-5759

It is a fact that very few politicians have the courage to propose such a controversial idea. A large membership in C.F.I.D.S. will provide the backing to move this plan forward.

IT'S UP TO YOU!

In the final analysis, the implementation of **THE DRUG SOLUTION** is up to you, the American public. Billions of your dollars are being spent by drug lords and fat cats. More of your money is being spent by drug enforcement agencies in trying to accomplish the impossible by attempting to enforce laws that can't be enforced. Your streets and neighborhoods are deteriorating both physically and socially. You do not have the benefit of a multi billion dollar industry. It's being robbed from you and your children. And what's more, this situation will never get better **UNLESS YOU ACT NOW!** Contact every Senator, Congressman, law enforcement agency, and personal acquaintance you know. Let them know how you feel about the ides in this book. The ramifications of acting or not acting are enormous. If we do nothing, we risk the status quo. Many indications are that this will end in bankrupting our country. We have spent billions on outlawing drugs with little or no positive results and disastrous negative results. We simply can't afford to continue to waste these resources.

If, on the other hand, we **ACT** to assure our leaders that this subject is not political suicide but a viable solution, we can be assured of a future with economic prosperity, social justice, and public safety.

It is time to implement **THE DRUG SOLUTION** as an alternative that will see us into to a bright and hopeful future.

APPENDIX

WHAT ELSE CAN YOU DO ABOUT DRUG USE IN AMERICA?

The author and *C.F.I.D.S.* in no way endorse the use of drugs, alcohol, or mind altering substances. We emphatically discourage their use. In an effort to distribute information that will help reduce the use of these substances *C.F.I.D.S.* is providing the following reprints and resources for the benefit of those who wish to obtain help for themselves or loved ones.

Printed by: **The Office for Substance Abuse Prevention.**

Distributed by: **The National Clearinghouse for Alcohol and Drug Information P.O. Box 2345 Rockville, MD 20852**

Americans have become concerned as never before about the dangers of alcohol and other drug use. Public opinion polls have repeatedly indicated a general intolerance for the use of alcohol by minors and the use of illegal drugs by anyone. Indicators show that most Americans are prepared to take a stand against such illegal alcohol and other drug use.

The abuse of alcohol and the use of illegal drugs have ravaged families, and have infiltrated our streets, neighborhoods, and schoolyards. These problems have also invaded the workplace and the highway. The American public has finally said, "We've had

195

enough," and is joining forces against drug use.

This section is designed to help all Americans meet that challenge. It provides vital information about alcohol and other drugs, their physiological effects, and how we can help each other overcome the problems alcohol and other drugs can cause. The first section explains what drugs are, how and why use starts, and the physical and psychological toll alcohol and other drugs take. After reading that material, you may want to know how to prevent alcohol and other drug problems among your family and friends, the topic of the next section.

There you will find information on early education and how to prevent problems before they start. You will also learn how you can set an example for those close to you and how you can teach children to resist pressure to use alcohol and other drugs. The section that follows explains how you can tell if someone you care about is having problems with alcohol and/or other drugs. This section not only explains the best steps to take to help, but also gives you pointers on what you should not do. The last section provides a list of federal, state, and private organizations you can turn to for help.

WHAT ARE DRUGS?

What Kinds of Drugs are There?

There are many drugs that affect the mind or behavior, and they are either legal or illegal. Legal drugs have been approved for sale either by prescription or over the counter. Alcohol, which is legally available in beverages except to those under legal drinking age, is a drug. Illegal drugs are those whose manufacture, sale, purchase for sale, or possession is prohibited by law. These include such drugs as marijuana, cocaine, PCP, and heroin or those drugs obtained by illegal means or used for illicit purposes. Prescription drugs are drugs that have been determined to be safe, effective, and legal only when given under the direction of a licensed physician. The manufacture and dispensing of prescription drugs is regulated by laws enforced by the Food and Drug Administration, the Drug Enforcement Administration, and the individual states. If used improperly, people can become physically dependent upon some prescription drugs (for example, morphine and valium.

Illegal drugs are sold and used without regard to the law. They may harm those who use them—not only in terms of the direct physical and emotional damage they cause, but also in terms of the criminal and financial consequences they bring. Many illegal drugs are manufactured in illegal underground laboratories in the United States.

How and Why Does Drug Use Start?

How and why do people start using alcohol and other drugs? There is no single answer to that question. Surely in the case of many youths, alcohol and other drug use starts in response to peer pressure. Young people naturally want to "fit in" to be accepted by their classmates or friends. Whatever the reasons, first use can be dangerous. Research studies show that once involvement with alcohol and other drugs begins, such involvement all too often follows a predictable sequence leading to problems due to the use of alcohol and other drugs.

Drug abuse often starts with the illicit use of legal drugs and with the use of alcohol (illegal for youth) and tobacco; users often progress from these substances to marijuana. Some users, including over half of the teenagers who use these substances, may eventually turn to other illegal drugs or combinations of drugs. For this reason, alcohol tobacco, and marijuana are frequently called "gateway" drugs. Use of drugs such as cocaine and heroin is unusual in those who have not previously used alcohol, tobacco, and/or marijuana.

What Are the Physical and Psychological Effects of Alcohol and Other Drugs?

Alcohol, a natural substance formed by the fermentation that occurs when sugar reacts with yeast, is the major active ingredient in wine, beer, and distilled spirits. Although there are many kinds of alcohol the kind found in alcoholic beverages is ethyl alcohol. Whether one drinks a 12-ounce can of beer, a shot (1.5 ounces) of distilled spirits, or a 5-ounce glass of wine, the amount of pure alcohol per drink is about the same one half ounce. Ethyl alcohol can produce feelings of well-being, sedation, intoxication, or unconsciousness, depending on the amount and the manner in which it is consumed.

Alcohol is a "psychoactive" or mind-altering drug, as are heroin and tranquilizers. It can alter moods, cause changes in the body, and become habit-forming. Alcohol is called a "downer" because it depresses the central nervous system. That's why drinking too much causes slowed reactions, slurred speech, and sometimes even unconsciousness (passing out). Alcohol initial effects are on the part of the brain that controls inhibitions.

A person does not have to be an alcoholic to have problems with alcohol. Every year, for example, many young people lose their lives in alcohol-related automobile crashes, drownings, and suicides. Serious health problems can and do occur before drinkers reach the stage of addiction or chronic use.

In some studies more than 25 percent of hospital admissions were alcohol-related Some of the serious diseases associated with chronic alcohol use include alcoholism and cancers of the liver, stomach, colon, larynx, esophagus, and breast.

Alcohol abuse also can lead to such serious physical problems as: High blood pressure, heart attacks, and strokes. Stomach and duodenal ulcers, colitis, and irritable colon. Use by pregnant women can cause birth defects and Fetal Alcohol Syndrome, whose effects include learning disabilities, low birth weight, small head size, and limb abnormalities. A host of other disorders, such as diminished immunity to disease, sleep disturbances, muscle cramps, and edema. can also be attributed to alcohol abuse.

Marijuana

Contrary to many young people's beliefs, marijuana is a harmful drug, especially since the potency of the marijuana now available has increased more than 275 percent over the last decade. For those who smoke marijuana now, the dangers are much more serious than they were in the 1960's. Preliminary studies have shown chronic lung disease in some marijuana users. There are more known cancer-causing agents in marijuana smoke than in cigarette smoke. In fact, because marijuana smokers try to hold the smoke in their lungs as long as possible, one marijuana cigarette can be as damaging to the lungs as four tobacco cigarettes. Even small doses of marijuana can impair memory function, distort perception, hamper judgment, and diminish motor skills.

Chronic marijuana use can cause brain damage and changes in the brain similar to those that occur during aging. Health effects also include accelerated heartbeat and, in some persons, increased blood pressure. These changes pose health risks for anyone, but particularly for people with abnormal heart and circulatory conditions, such as high blood pressure and hardening of the arteries. Marijuana can also have a serious effect on reproduction. Studies have shown that women who smoke marijuana during pregnancy may give birth to babies with defects similar to those seen in infants born with Fetal Alcohol Syndrome—for example, low body weight and small heads.

More importantly, there is increasing concern about how marijuana use by children and adolescents affects both their short- and long-term development. Mood changes occur with the first use. Observers in clinical settings have noted increased apathy, loss of ambition, loss of effectiveness, diminished ability to carry out long-term plans, difficulty in concentrating, and a decline in school or work performance. Many teenagers who end up in drug treatment programs started using marijuana at an early age.

Driving under the influence of marijuana is especially dangerous. Marijuana impairs driving skills for at least 4 to 6 hours after smoking a single cigarette. When marijuana is used in combination with alcohol driving skills become even more impaired.

Cocaine

Cocaine is one of the most powerfully addictive of the drugs of abuse—and it is a drug that can kill. No individual can predict whether he or she will become addicted or whether the next dose of cocaine will prove fatal. Cocaine can be snorted through the nose, smoked, or injected. Injecting cocaine or injecting any drug carries the added risk of infection with the Human Immunodeficiency Virus (HIV), the virus that causes Acquired Immunodeficiency Syndrome (AIDS).

Cocaine is a very strong stimulant to the central nervous system, including the brain. This drug produces an accelerated heart rate while at the same time constricting the blood vessels, which are trying to handle the additional flow of blood. Pupils dilate and temperature and blood pressure rise.These physical changes may be accompanied by seizures, cardiac arrest, respiratory arrest, or stroke. Nasal problems, including congestion and a runny nose, occur with the use of cocaine, and with prolonged use the mucous membrane of the nose may disintegrate. Heavy cocaine use can sufficiently damage the nasal septum to cause it to collapse.

Research has shown that cocaine acts directly on what have been called the "pleasure centers" in the brain. These "pleasure centers" are brain structures that, when stimulated, produce an intense desire to experience the pleasure effects again and again. This causes changes in brain activity and, by allowing a brain chemical called dopamine to remain active longer than normal triggers an intense craving for more of the drug. Users often report feelings of restlessness, irritability, and anxiety, and cocaine can trigger paranoia. Users also report being depressed when they are not using the drug and often resume use to alleviate further depression.

In addition, cocaine users frequently find that they need more and more cocaine more often to generate the same level of stimulation. Therefore, any use can lead to addiction.

"Freebase" is a form of cocaine that is smoked. "Freebase" is produced by a chemical process whereby "street cocaine" (cocaine hydrochloride) is converted to a pure base by removing the hydrochloride salt and some of the "cutting" agents. The end product is not water soluble, and so the only way to get it into the system is to smoke it. "Freebasing" is extremely dangerous. The cocaine reaches the brain within seconds, resulting in a sudden and intense high. However, the euphoria quickly disappears, leaving the user with an enormous craving to freebase again and again. The user usually increases the dose and the frequency to satisfy this craving, resulting in addiction and physical debilitation.

"Crack" is the street name given to one form of freebase cocaine that comes in the form of small lumps or shavings. The term "crack" refers to the crackling sound made when the mixture is smoked (heated). Crack has become a major problem in many American cities because it is inexpensive selling for between $5 and $10 for one or two doses and easily transportable sold in small vials, folding paper, or tinfoil.

PCP

PCP is a hallucinogenic drug; that is, a drug that alters sensation, mood, and consciousness and that distorts hearing, touch, smell, or taste as well as visual sensation. It is legitimately used as an anaesthetic for animals. When used by humans, PCP induces a profound departure from reality, which leaves the user capable of bizarre behavior and severe disorientation. These PCP-induced effects may lead to serious injuries or death to the user while under the influence of the drug.

PCP produces feelings of mental depression in some individuals. When PCP is used regularly, memory, perception functions, concentration, and judgment are often disturbed. Used chronically, PCP may lead to permanent changes in cognitive ability (thinking), memory, and fine motor function.

Mothers using PCP during pregnancy often deliver babies who have visual, auditory, and motor disturbances. These babies may also have sudden outbursts of agitation and other rapid changes in awareness similar to the responses in adults intoxicated with PCP.

Heroin

Heroin is an illegal opiate drug. Its addictive properties are manifested by the need for persistent, repeated use of the drug (craving) and by the fact that attempts to stop using the drug lead to significant and painful physical withdrawal symptoms. Use of heroin causes physical and psychological problems such as shallow breathing, nausea, panic, insomnia, and a need for increasingly higher doses of the drug to get the same effect. Heroin exerts its primary addictive effect by activating many regions of the brain; the brain regions affected are responsible for producing both the pleasurable sensation of "reward" and physical dependence. Together, these actions account for the user's loss of control and the drug's habit-forming action.

Heroin is a drug that is primarily taken by injection (a shot) with a needle in the vein. This form of use is called intravenous injection (commonly known as IV injection). This means of drug entry can have grave consequences. Uncertain dosage levels (due to differences in purity), the use of unsterile equipment, contamination of heroin with cutting agents, or the use of heroin in combination with such other drugs as alcohol or cocaine can cause serious health problems such as serum hepatitis, skin abscesses, inflammation of the veins, and cardiac disease (subacute bacterial endocarditis).

Of great importance, however, is that the user never knows whether the next dose will be unusually potent, leading to overdose, coma, and possible death.

Needle sharing by IV drug users is fast becoming the leading cause of new AIDS cases. It is estimated that one in three persons with AIDS acquired the virus through needle sharing.

The AIDS virus is carried in contaminated blood left in the needle, syringe, or other drug-related implements and is injected into the new user when he or she uses this equipment to inject heroin or other drugs. There is no cure for AIDS and no proven vaccine to prevent it.

Heroin use during pregnancy is associated with stillbirths and miscarriages. Babies born addicted to heroin must undergo withdrawal after birth and these babies show a number of developmental problems.

The signs and symptoms of heroin use include euphoria, drowsiness, respiratory depression (which can progress until breathing stops), constricted pupils, and nausea. Withdrawal symptoms include watery eyes, runny nose, yawning, loss of appetite, tremors, panic, chills, sweating, nausea, muscle cramps, and insomnia. Elevations in blood pressure, pulse, respiratory rate, and temperature occur as withdrawal progresses. Symptoms of a heroin overdose include shallow breathing, pinpoint pupils, clammy skin, convulsions, and coma.

Analogs

By modifying the chemical structure of certain drugs to create analogs, underground chemists have been able to create what are sometimes called "designer drugs"—a common label that incorrectly glamorizes them. These analogs are chemicals structurally similar to medical drugs but which are altered enough to make them different compounds. They are on the Drug Enforcement Administration's (DEA) list of controlled substances. Originally, analogs were designed to circumvent the Controlled Substances Act, but in 1984 and 1986, all "designer drugs" were added to the list of controlled substances.

Examples of designer drugs are an analog of methamphetamine (commonly called **"ecstasy"**) and an analog of fentanyl (a narcotic). These drugs are made in underground laboratories with no regard for cleanliness or quality. Thus, these drugs can be much more potent than the original substances, and they can therefore produce much more toxic effects.

Methamphetamine

Methamphetamine is a powerful stimulant. The street version of the drug is most often manufactured illegally in underground labs. It is also known as "speed" or "crystal" when it is swallowed or sniffed; as "crank" when it is injected; and as "ice" when it is smoked. All forms are extremely dangerous. Side effects of methamphetamine use include irritability, nervousness, insomnia, nausea, hot flashes, dryness of the mouth, sweating, palpitations, and hypertension. Excessive doses can produce mental confusion, severe anxiety, and aggressiveness. Continued moderate to chronic use may lead to physical dependence and even death.

THE EFFECTS OF ALCOHOL

THE BRAIN

Brain cells are altered, and may die. Memory formation is blocked, and the senses are dulled. In the long term, irreversible damage occurs.

STOMACH & INTESTINES
Alcohol can trigger bleeding, and has been linked to cancer.

CEREBELLUM
Physical coordination is impaired.

HEART
Deterioration of the heart muscle can occur.

THE IMMUNE SYSTEM
Infection fighting cells are prevented from function properly, and the risk of viral or bacterial diseases is increased.

REPRODUCTION
In men hormone levels change, causing lower sex drive and enlarged breasts. Women's menstrual cycles become irregular, and their ovaries malfunction. Pregnant women face the risk of bearing children with birth defects.

THE LIVER
The liver suffers more than any other organ. It filters most of the alcohol out of the bloodstream and breaks it down.
Because of its high caloric content, alcohol displaces key nutrients, sometimes causing malnutrition. Excess calories are stored in the liver as fat. This is one of the earliest signs of alcoholic liver disease. Eventually the liver cells die resulting in cirrhosis, a degeneration of the organ.

THE PROBLEM OF DRUG ABUSE

How Can I Tell If Someone I Know Is Using Drugs?

Aside from the physical effects of drugs discussed in the preceding section, certain warning signs may indicate that a family member or friend is drinking too much alcohol or using other drugs. Although these warning signs are not foolproof, each by itself or many signs combined over time should be cause for concern.

These are some of the signs to look for which involve drinking:

- Does the person drink until intoxicated?
- Does the person drive a car while intoxicated?
- Does he or she handle all social celebrations and stress with alcohol?

These are the signs of an adult problem drinker. It is important to note, however, that any use of alcohol by youth is abuse and cause for concern. Young abusers become addicted in as little as six months as opposed to adults who often take years to become addicted to alcohol. When these signs are present, it means that a person's drinking pattern, if not already out of control, is heading that way. A person does not have to be an alcoholic to have problems with alcohol.

There are numerous signs of illegal drug use. For example, when a person is carrying drugs or has them hidden around the house, there is a strong possibility of use. Obviously, possession of drug paraphernalia also is a likely sign of use. Indications of prescription drug misuse vary according to the type of drug in question. Drug misuse may lead to dependence and withdrawal symptoms can be severe if drug use is stopped suddenly.

Certain additional behavioral characteristics also seem to accompany the use of alcohol and other drugs. The clues can be found in all people who abuse alcohol or use other drugs, regardless of age.

Examples of these clues include:

- Sudden and continuing decline in attendance or performance at work or in school.
- Impaired relationships with family members or friends.
- Increased amount and frequency of borrowing money from family and friends.
- Heightened secrecy about actions and possessions.

What to do.

Be Understanding— listen to reasons why he or she uses/abuses alcohol or other drugs;

Be Supportive—assist the user in finding help and provide moral support through the tough times ahead;

Don't be sarcastic, stigmatizing, or blaming.

Intervening in the case of a family member or friend who has a problem can be very difficult and hurtful. The person with the problem will most likely deny the problem and try to put you on the defensive—"I thought you were my friend; are you calling me a drunk.?" Or

"You've used drugs; where do you get off calling me an addict?" In a case such as this, what you don't do is as important as what you should do:

Don't cover up or make excuses for the person.

Don't argue with the person when he or she is under the influence of alcohol or other drugs.

Above all, don't accept responsibility for the persons's actions nor guilt for his or her drinking.

Four Basic Stages of Alcohol and Other Drug Use

Stage 1

Too many youngsters and adults believe that the first use of alcohol and other drugs is safe. For youths, using drugs such as tobacco and alcohol is often, unfortunately, viewed as normal. However, because young bodies are particularly susceptible to alcohol and other drugs and their effects, there is no such thing as totally "safe" use of any mind-altering drug by a youngster. In stage one, however, there may be no outward behavioral changes caused by the use of drugs.

Stage 2

The second stage involves more frequent use of alcohol or other drugs as the person actively seeks the euphoric effects of a mind-altering drug. At this point, the user usually establishes a reliable source, and may add mid-week use of alcohol or other drugs to previous habits of weekend use at parties.

Among adolescents, significant clues now include changes in friends, deterioration of school performance, and possibly a general lack of motivation.

Stage 3

In stage three, there is intense preoccupation with the desire to experience euphoric effects. Daily use of mind-altering drugs, depression, and thoughts of suicide are common. Family troubles increase and the adolescent may be having problems with the law.

Stage 4

In the fourth stage, increasing amounts of alcohol are needed just to feel OK. Physical signs such as coughing, frequent sore throats, weight loss, and fatigue—which may have begun to appear earlier— are now common.

Blackouts and overdosing also are more common, family life is a disaster, and crime may be becoming a way of life to obtain money to buy drugs.

How Can I Keep My Family Free From Problems Caused By

ALCOHOL AND OTHER DRUGS?

What Early Education Information Do I Need?

Knowledge is a powerful weapon against drugs. The information contained in this pamphlet represents a good start in your educational efforts. However, to increase your understanding of drugs and their effects, you should also read some additional material. In addition to some excellent information available from private sources, the Federal Government has compiled a great deal of information about the effects of alcohol abuse and other drug use and the successful strategies that can be used to combat these problems. Free materials may be obtained by writing to:

The National Clearinghouse for Alcohol and Drug Information, P.O. Box 2345, Rockville, Maryland 20852 or you may want to call the Clearinghouse's toll-free number: 1 (800) SAY-NO-TO(DRUGS).

How Can I Set an Example?

First and foremost, set an example by not using illegal drugs or misusing alcohol or prescription drugs. Period. No excuses or self-exceptions should be offered to yourself or to others. If alcohol is used it should be used only by persons of legal age and only in moderation. Prescription drugs should only be used when prescribed and closely monitored by a physician. And you should abstain from the use of any illegal drugs.

Don't keep illegal drugs in the house and don't allow their use in your home by others. Let your family and friends know that drugs are not acceptable in your home. And let others know that you do not tolerate illegal drugs at parties that you or your family attend. Talk to your neighbors about the fact that drug use should not be tolerated on your streets or anywhere else near you.

The best way to keep your family from abusing alcohol (any use of alcohol by youth is abuse) is by carefully looking at the example set in your home. Are your parties, entertainment, and celebrations centered around alcohol? Do you reach for a drink or another drug whenever you want to relax or to deal with any problem that comes up? Such behavior sends the wrong signal that alcohol and other drugs are needed to have a good time or to cope with daily living.

How Can I Help My Younger Children To Say "No"?

First, talk to your child about alcohol and other drugs. carefully explain the health consequences of alcohol and other drug use, and the dramatic effect they can have on a child's life and preparation for the future. Correct mistaken ideas perpetuated by peers and the media. And really listen carefully to your child talk about alcohol and other drugs. Children are more likely to communicate when they receive positive verbal and nonverbal cues that show parents are listening.

Second, help your child to develop a healthy self-image. Self regard is enhanced when parents praise effort as well as accomplishments. In turn, when being critical, criticize the actions and not the person.

Third, help your child develop a strong system of values. A strong value system can give children the criteria and courage to make decisions based on facts rather than pressure from friends.

Fourth, help your child deal with peer pressure. Explain that saying "No" can be an important statement about self worth. Help your child practice saying "No." Together, set out the reasons for saying "No" and discuss why it is beneficial to avoid alcohol and other drugs.

Fifth, make family policies that help your child to say "No." The strongest support your child can have in refusing to use alcohol and other drugs is to be found in the solid bonds created within the family unit. Always chaperone your children's parties. It is helpful when parents let other family members—and friends—know that drug use, and use of alcohol by minors, is a violation of the rules by which the family will operate, and that their use of alcohol and other drugs is simply unacceptable within the family. The consequences and punishment for such a violation must be clearly spelled out.

Sixth, encourage your child to join an anti-drug club. With over 10,000 clubs nationwide, chances are that your child's school has such a club. If not, it might be a good idea to contact the local principal about starting a club. These clubs help develop positive peer pressure, strengthening children's ability to say "No," and the clubs teach the harmful effects of alcohol and other drugs on children's bodies.

Finally, encourage healthy, creative activities that may help to prevent children from using alcohol and other drugs. Help your child live such a full life that there is no time nor place for alcohol and other drugs. Meet the parents of your child's friends and classmates and encourage alcohol and other drug-free alternative activities. Learn about drugs and share "no use" message of alcohol or other drugs for youth. Discuss guidelines and problem areas and agree to keep in touch.

Consider forming parent-peer groups. There is strength in numbers. Making these contacts before there is a problem often prevents the problem from ever developing. When the entire peer group is on the right track, you stand a better chance of keeping your child drug free.

Where Can I Go For Help?

Sometimes the quickest way to find out what help is available in your local area is to join a group such as Al-Anon. Al-Anon is a group of family members and friends of problem drinkers who meet to share practical suggestions on day-to-day living with someone who has a drinking problem. These family members and friends of problem drinkers usually know where help is available in your community.

Other publications available in the Drug-Free Communities Series:
Drug Free Communities:
Turning Awareness Into Action

A booklet that examines the cultural and community attitudes, norms, and environmental factors that encourage the use of alcohol and other drugs. Persons interested in prevention who are looking for help in getting started.

Prevention Plus 2:
Tools for Creating and Sustaining a Drug-Free Community

A technical assistance manual for organizing or expanding community alcohol and other drug prevention activities for youth into a coordinated, complementary system. Written for persons from throughout the community who are in a position to assist in organizing a prevention effort.

Citizens' Alcohol and Other Drug Prevention Directory:
Resources for Getting Involved

For information on where to find treatment for alcohol and other drug problems, the best place to look is in the telephone book's Yellow Pages under "Alcoholism Information" or "Drug Abuse and Addiction Information." Usually there is a listing of the nearest Council on Alcoholism (or Council on Alcohol and Drug Abuse). These Councils provide information over the phone on the availability of the nearest alcohol treatment programs. Alcoholics Anonymous (AA) or Narcotics Anonymous (NA) may also be listed. Both offer immeasurable help in helping people to cope with problems with alcohol and other drugs.

For further information, write to:

National Clearinghouse for
Alcohol and Drug Information
P.O. Box 2345
Rockville, Maryland 20852
or call:
1-800-729-6686

This directory, developed to serve as an aid to citizens interested in learning more about prevention, lists a wide variety of prevention services and prevention activities. With this guide, every American will have the information needed to call or write to all of the major organizations in the prevention field for assistance, information, or resources.

Listed below are some other sources of help and information:

1-800-SAY-NO-TO(DRUGS)
National Clearinghouse for
Alcohol and Drug Information
Monday through Friday,
8:30 a.m. - 5:00 p.m.

1-800-622-HELP
National Institute on Drug
Abuse Information and
Referral Line
Monday through Friday,
8:30 a.m. - 4:30 p.m.

1-800-554-KIDS
The National Federation of
Parents for Drug-Free Youth
Monday through Friday,
9:00 a.m. - 5:00 p.m.

1-800-622-2255
National Council on Alcoholism
7 days a week, 24 hours a day.

1-800-241-9746
Parent's Resource Institute
for Drug Education (PRIDE)
Monday through Friday,
8:30 a.m. - 5:00 p.m.
(Recorded service other
times)

1-800-COCAINE
Cocaine Helpline
Monday through Friday,
9:00 a.m. - 3.00 a.m.
Saturday and Sunday,
12:00 p.m. - 3:00 a.m.

1-800-843-4971
The National Institute on
Drug Abuse Workplace Helpline
(For employers establishing
workplace drug abuse programs)
Monday through Friday,
9:00 a.m. - 8:00 p.m.

OTHER RESOURCES

PRIVATE ORGANIZATIONS, CIVIC GROUPS, RELIGIOUS ORGANIZATIONS

Adult Children of Alcoholics(ACoA)
P.O. Box 3216
Torrance, CA 90505
(213) 534-1815

Al-Anon Family Groups
P.O. Box 862
Midtown Station
New York, NY 10018
(212) 302-7240

Alcoholics Anonymous (AA)
15 E. 26th Street Rm. 1810
New York, NY 10010
(212) 683-3900

American Council for Drug Education
204 Monroe Street
Suite 110
Rockville, MD 20850
(301) 294-0600

The Chemical People/WQED
4802 Fifth Avenue
Pittsburgh, PA 15213
(412) 622-1491

Coalition of Hispanic Health
and Human Services
Organizations (COSSMHO)
1030 15th Street, NW,
Suite 1053
Washington, DC 20005
(202) 371-2100

Cocaine Anonymous (CA)
3740 Overland Ave.
Suite G
Los Angeles, CA 90034
1(800) 347-8998

CoAnon Family Groups
P.O. Box 64742-66
Los Angeles, CA 90064
(213) 859-2206

Families Anonymous, Inc.
P.O. Box 548
Van Nuys, CA 91408
(818) 989-7841

Institute on Black Chemical Abuse
2614 Nicollet Avenue
Minneapolis, MN 55408
(612) 871-7878

Just Say No Foundation
1777 North California Blvd.
Room 210
Walnut Creek, CA 94596
(415) 939-6666

Mothers Against Drunk Driving
511 E. John Carpenter Freeway
Suite 700
Irving, TX 75062
(214) 744-6233

Nar-Anon Family Groups
P.O. Box 2562
Palos Verdes Peninsula, CA
90274
(213) 547-5800

Narcotics Anonymous (NA)
P.O. Box 9999
Van Nuys, CA 91409
(818) 780-3951

National Asian Pacific
American Families Against
Drug Abuse
6303 Friendship Court
Bethesda, MD 20817
(301) 530-0945

National Association for
Children of Alcoholics
(NACoA)
31582 Coast Highway
Suite B
South Laguna, CA 92677
(714) 499-3889

National Association of
State Alcohol and Drug Abuse

Directors (NASADAD)
444 N. Capitol Street, NW
Suite 642
Washington, DC 20001
(202) 783-6868

National Black Alcoholism
Council (NBAC)
1629 K Street, N.W.
Suite 802
Washington, D.C. 20006
(202) 296-2696

National Families in Action
2296 Henderson Mill Road
Suite 204
Atlanta, GA 30345
(404) 934-6364

National Federation of
Parents for Drug-Free Youth
1423 North Jefferson
Springfield, MO 65802
(417) 836-3709

National Parents Resource
Institute for Drug Education
(PRIDE)
The Hurt Building
Suite 210
Hurt Plaza
Atlanta, GA 30303
(404) 651-2548

National Prevention Network
444 North Capitol Street, NW
Suite 642
Washington, DC 20001
(202) 783-6868

Quest International
537 Jones Road
P.O. Box 566
Grandville, OH 43023
(614) 587-2800

Women for Sobriety
P.O. Box 618
Quakertown, PA 18951
(215) 536-8026

STATE ORGANIZATIONS

Alabama
Division of Mental Illness
and Substance Abuse
Community Programs
Department of Mental Health
200 Interstate Park Drive
P.O. Box 3710
Montgomery 36193
(205) 271-9250

Alaska
Office of Alcoholism and Drug Abuse
Department of Health &
Social Services
Pouch H-05-F
Juneau 99811
(907) 586-6201

Arizona
Alcoholism and Drug Abuse
Office of Comm. Behav. Health
Dept. of Health Services
411 N. 24th Street
Phoenix 85008
(602) 220-6455

Arkansas
Office on Alcohol and Drug
Abuse Prevention
Donaghey Plaza, North
Suite 400
P.O. Box 1437
Little Rock 72203-1437
(501) 682-6650

California
Department of Alcohol
and Drug Programs
111 Capitol Mall
Suite 450
Sacramento 95814
(916) 445-0834

Colorado
Alcohol and Drug Abuse Div.
Department of Health
4210 East 11th Avenue
Denver 80220
(303) 331-8201

Connecticut
Connecticut Alcohol and Drug
Abuse Commission
999 Asylum Avenue, 3rd Floor
Hartford 06105
(203) 566-4145

Delaware
Delaware Division of Alcoholism,
Drug Abuse and Mental Health
1901 N. DuPont Highway
Newcastle 19720
(302) 421-6101

District of Columbia
Health Planning and Dev.

1660 L Street, NW
Washington 20036
(202) 673-7481

Florida
Alcohol and Drug Abuse Program
Department of Health and
Rehabilitative Services
1317 Winewood Boulevard
Tallahassee 32301
(904) 488-0900

Georgia
Alcohol and Drug Services
878 Peachtree Street, NE.,
Suite 318
Atlanta 30309
(404) 8946352

Hawaii
Alcohol and Drug Abuse Div.
Department of Health
P.O. Box 3378
Honolulu 96801
(808) 548-4280

Idaho
Dept. of Health and Welfare
450 West State Street
Boise 83720
(208) 3345935

Illinois
Department of Alcoholism
and Substance Abuse
100 West Randolph Street
Suite 5-600
Chicago 60601
(312) 8-14384

Indiana
Division of Addiction Services
Department of Mental Health
117 East Washington Street
Indianapolis 46204
(317) 232-7816

Iowa
Department of Public Health
Division of Substance Abuse
and Health Promotion
Lucas State Office Building
4th Floor
Des Moines 50319
(515) 281-3641

Kansas
Alcohol and Drug Abuse Services
300 S.W. Oakley
Biddle Building
Topeka 66606-1861
(913) 296-3925

Kentucky
Division of Substance Abuse
Department for Mental Health
and Mental Retardation
Services
275 East Main Street
Frankfort 40621
(502) 564-2880

Louisiana
Office of Human Services
Div. of Alcohol and Drug
Abuse
1201 Capitol Access Road
P.O. Box 3868
Baton Rouge 70821-3868
(504) 342-9354

Maine
Office of Alcoholism and Drug
Abuse Prevention
Bureau of Rehabilitation
State House Station #11
Augusta 04333
(207) 289-2781

Maryland
Maryland State Alcohol and
Drug Abuse Administration
201 West Preston Street
Baltimore 21201
(301) 225-6925

Massachusetts
Div. of Substance Abuse Services
150 Tremont Street
Boston 02111
(617) 727-8614

Michigan
Off. of Substance Abuse Services
Department of Public Health
2150 Apollo Drive
P.O. Box 30206
Lansing 48909
(517) 335-8809

Minnesota
Chemical Dependency
Program Division
Department of Human Services
444 Lafayette Road
St. Paul 55155-3823
(612) 296-4610

Mississippi
Div. of Alcohol and Drug Abuse

Department of Mental Health
Robert E. Lee State Office
Building, 11th Floor
Jackson 39201
(601) 359-1288

Missouri
Div. of Alcohol and Drug Abuse
Department of Mental Health
1915 South Ridge Drive
P.O. Box 687
Jefferson City 65102
(314) 751-4942

Montana
Alcohol and Drug Abuse Div.
Department of Institutions
Helena 59601
(406) 444-2827

Nebraska
Div. of Alcoholism and Drug Abuse
Department of Public Inst.
P.O. Box 94728
Lincoln 68509
(402) 471-2851, Ext. 5583

Nevada
Alcohol & Drug Abuse Bureau
Dept. Human Resources
505 East King Street
Carson City 89710
(702) 885-4790

New Hampshire
Office of Alcohol and Drug
Abuse Prevention
Health and Welfare Building
Hazen Drive

Concord 03301
(603) 271-4627

New Jersey
Department of Health
CN 360
Trenton 08625
(609) 292-3147

Division of Narcotic and Drug Abuse Control
129 East Hanover Street
Trenton 08625
(609) 292-5760

New Mexico
Substance Abuse Bureau
190 St. Francis Drive
Room 3350 North
Santa Fe 87503
(505) 827-2589

New York
Division of Alcoholism and Alcohol Abuse
194 Washington Avenue
Albany 12210
(518) 474-5417

Div. of Substance Abuse Services
Executive Park S., Box 8200
Albany 12203
(518) 457-7629

North Carolina
Alcohol and Drug Abuse Section
Division of Mental Health and
Mental Retardation Services
325 North Salisbury Street
Raleigh 27611
(919) 733-4670

North Dakota
Division of Alcoholism and Drug Abuse
Dept. of Human Services
State Capitol/Judicial Wing
Bismarck 58505
(701) 224-2769

Ohio
Bureau on Alcohol Abuse and Recovery
Ohio Department of Health
170 North High Street,
3rd Fl.
Columbus 43266-0586
(614) 466-3445

Bureau on Drug Abuse
Ohio Department of Health
170 N. High Street, 3rd Floor
Columbus 43266-0586
(614) 466-7893

Oklahoma
Oklahoma Department of Mental Health and
Substance Abuse Services
P.O. Box 53277
Capitol Station
Oklahoma City 73152
(405) 271-7474

Oregon
Office of Alcohol and Drug Abuse Programs
1178 Chemeketa Street, NE, #102
Salem 97310
(503) 378-2163

Pennsylvania
Drug and Alcohol Programs
PA Department of Health
P.O. Box 90
Harrisburg 17108

(717) 787-9857

Rhode Island
Division of Substance Abuse
Department of Mental Health,
Retardation and Hospitals
P.O. Box 20363
Cranston 02920
(401) 464-2091

South Carolina
South Carolina Commission on
Alcohol and Drug Abuse
3700 Forest Drive
Columbia 29204
(803) 734-9520

South Dakota
Div. of Alcohol and Drug Abuse
Joe Foss Building
523 East Capitol
Pierre 57501
(605) 773-3123

Tennessee
Alcohol and Drug Abuse Services
Dept. of Mental Health and
Mental Retardation
706 Church Street, 4th Floor
Nashville 37219
(615) 741-1921

Texas
Texas Commission on Alcohol
and Drug Abuse
1705 Guadalupe Street
Austin 78701
(512) 463-5510

Utah

Division of Substance Abuse
Department of Social Services
120 N. 200 West, 4th Floor
P.O. Box 45500
Salt Lake City, 84145-0500
(801) 538-3939

Vermont
Office of Alcohol and Drug
Abuse Programs
103 South Maine Street
Waterbury 05676
(802) 241-2170/241-2175

Virginia
Off. of Substance Abuse Services
Dept. of Mental Health,
Mental Retardation and
Substance Services
P.O. Box 1797
109 Governor Street
Richmond 23214
(804) 786-3906

Washington
Bureau of Alcoholism and Substance Abuse
Washington Department of
Social and Health Services
Mail Stop OB-44W
Olympia 98504
(206) 753-5866

West Virginia
Div. of Alcohol and Drug Abuse
State Capitol
1800 Washington Street, East,
Room 451
Charleston 25305
(304) 348-2276

Wisconsin
Office of Alcohol and Other Drug Abuse
1 West Wilson Street
P.O. Box 7851
Madison 53707
(608) 266-3442

Wyoming
Alcohol and Drug Abuse Programs
Hathaway Building
Cheyenne 82002
(307) 777-7115, Ext. 7118

Guam
Department of Mental Health
and Substance Abuse
P.O. Box 9400
Tamuning 96911
(671) 646-9262-69

Puerto Rico
Dept. of Anti-Addiction Services
Box 21414
Rio Piedras Station
Rio Piedras 00928-1414
(809) 764-3795

Virgin Islands
Div. of Mental Health Alcoholism
and Drug Dependency Services
P.O. Box 520
St. Croix 00820
(809) 773-1992

American Samoa
Social Services Division
Alcohol and Drug Program
Government of American Samoa
Pago Pago 96799

Public Health Services
LBJ Tropical Medical Center
Pago Pago 96799

SOURCE NOTES

Bibliography

Abadinsky, Howard, Drug Abuse (1989);

Abadinsky, Howard, Organized Crime, .(1990);

Arterburn, Stephen, Growing Up Addicted (1989);

Bynum, T. S., ed., Organized Crime in America (1985);

Currie, Elliott, Reckoning: Drugs, The American Cities Future (1992);

Falco, Mathea, The Making of a Drug-Free America (1992);

Garrett, R. C., et al., The Coke Book (1984);

Gold, M. S., 800-Cocaine (1984);

Goode, Erich, Drugs in American Society, 3rd ed. (1988);

Greenhaven Press, Chemical Dependancy Opposing Viewpoints;

Greenhaw, Flying High (1989) Dodd Meade & CO;

Grilly, David M., Drugs and Human Behavior (1989);

Johnson, B. D., et al., Taking Care of Business: The Ecnomics of Crime by Heroin Users (1985)

Mc Williams, Peter, Ain't Nobody's Business If You Do. (1993) Prelude Press

Musto, David F., The American Disease: Control (1987);

O'Brien, Robert, and Cohen, Sidney, The Encyclopedia of Drug Abuse (1984);

Ray, Oakley, Drugs, Society, and Human Behavior, 3d ed. (1983);

Smith, D. C., The Mafia Mystique (1990).

Sugarman, Barry, and Spindler, George, The Great Drug War (1987);

Terkel, Should Drugs Be Legalized?(1990);

Weil, Andrew, and Rosen, Winifred, Chocolate to Morphine: Understanding Mind Active Drugs (1983);

COMPUSERVE COMPUTER SERVICES (1993)

U.S. DEPT OF JUSTICE BUREAU OF JUSTICE STATISTICS

Criminal Victimization it the U.S. (1990), and (1991)

Drugs and Crime Facts. (1992)

U.S. Dept of Health and Human Services.

Center for Substance Abuse Prevention (CSAP)

The National Clearinghouse for Alcohol and Drug Information (NCADI)

The National Institute on Drug Abuse (NIDA)

The Substance Abuse Information Database (SAID)